Miracles Never Ending

—— PRAISE ——

"Bob Canton has authored a very interesting, informative, and inspiring book, *Miracles Never Ending*. Bob's sincerity, joy, and zeal come through each page of this book. His personal testimony of experiencing the Baptism in the Holy Spirit is as amazing as it is humorous! Bob and his wife, Chita, were truly surprised by the Holy Spirit on November 11, 1984, and their lives have never been the same since. This book includes numerous healing testimonies from people Bob has ministered to in countries all over the world. In addition, Bob shares, with honesty and humility, principles he has learned about how to pray for healing. Having witnessed Bob's ministry first-hand, we can say that he manifests a great pastoral love and kindness toward those who come for prayer. Bob's concern is to lift up the Lord Jesus Christ and to allow Him to act in people's lives. Bob is a dear friend and brother in the Lord; we rejoice with him at the publication of this book."

—Al and Patti Mansfield—
Liaisons for the Charismatic Renewal
Archdiocese of New Orleans

"Bob Canton, in his ordinary, faithful Catholic life experienced the life changing Baptism of the Holy Spirit. From the early days of his family's involvement in Catholic

Praise

Charismatic Renewal, Bob learned how to grow as a disciple and move in the charismatic gifts. This subsequently led to him having an international ministry travelling to more than fifty countries ministering through healing, deliverance, and miracles. In this book he encourages everyone in the Church to be open to the Holy Spirit and to be a miracle worker in whatever area the Lord leads them.

This book manages very successfully to do several things. It is inspirational and faith building. It also presents teaching about the healing ministry, particularly within the context of the Catholic Church. Then, by sharing some helpful practical tips, Bob encourages everyone to step out in mission. The final chapters share some of the fruits of the ministry of healing and miracles and include many moving personal testimonies of specific healings.

I am sure this book, which tells of the mighty deeds of the Lord, will be a source of encouragement to everyone."

—Michelle Moran—
President, Vatican-based International
Catholic Charismatic
Renewal Services (ICCRS)

"Miracles Never Ending made me laugh, cry, and ponder how the Holy Spirit can change the lives of ordinary people. This book is going to give people hope and fill their hearts with faith.

I have witnessed Bob working for the Lord many times over the years I have known him, but in 2009 he visited

Arizona, at Queen of Peace Catholic Church, where many people were healed and many more received the gift of faith. Jesus is the healer, and the healings through Bob's preaching and praying over so many of the sick who came to that prayer rally were incredible.

Bob tells the story about how the Lord called him, an unsuspecting ordinary lay person, to go out and preach the Gospel all over the world. Jesus told Bob that He (Jesus) was going to use him to heal millions in His name. Bob's initial thoughts to this calling were, *Who, me? A sinner?*

I spoke with Bob about the similarities of the Bible story of Saul, who was also called by God, and how the entire course of his life changed. Saul, too, saw himself as a great sinner, but God saw something in him and called him to a significant mission, and God changed his name to Paul. Jesus also changed Bob's name from Robert to Rober; he has truly been called by the Lord to be His hands, His feet, His voice, and His heart. Lucky for all of us that Bob said Yes to God's will, much like the Blessed Mother did.

Bob didn't think that he would ever write a book, but wherever he goes, he is asked by many, "Why don't you write a book?". What you hold in your hands is the result. His book will touch many lives and bring love, peace, and joy to many."

— Sally Ann Quinones, Author —
Everlasting Grace

Praise

∞

"Every person involved in the Charismatic Renewal should have a copy of this book in his/her library. It is a book that I personally have been waiting for, from a holy man who has been called to a mission of healing, teaching, and evangelization, and who has impacted me and my family through his Healing Rallies and evangelistic activities that he has brought to people all over the world.

This book chronicles the experiences and adventures of a man who responded positively and in deep faith to the divine call, "Whom shall I send?" It is autobiographical with respect to his "divine encounter" and his "calling." This book gathers together in one place all of the author's teachings on healing and on Jesus and the Holy Spirit. Believing that most, if not all, people can likewise bring healing through prayer, the author has included pages on how to pray for healing with samples of his prayers tailored to specific diseases. Most remarkable is the number and variety of testimonies of healing coming from grateful people all over the world and covering a wide variety of illnesses. Medical scientists might argue this book's definition of "healing" (which doctors might rather call "remission" or "survival rate"), but when a sick person claims and feels that he/she is "healed" and rejoices and thanks the Lord for it, that definition should be accepted as real for that person. And this book is full of such testimonies.

Praise

Reading through this book will awaken in the reader the belief that indeed Jesus is alive—in history, in the present, and way into the future."
—Narciso S. Albarracin, Jr., M.D.—
Pathologist (retired) and former
Chair and Medical Director
Department of Pathology and
Laboratory Medicine
Doctors Hospital Ohio Health
Columbus, OH

"Bob's book is inspiring and informative. His experiences with our Lord are beyond fascinating. His book will lift you up, wake you up, and amaze you with real life examples of multitudes of people who have received healings in today's world from Jesus, the Divine Healer. I have witnessed Bob in action at several venues over the years. He is a compelling presenter. Bob also gives practical advice for anyone seeking healing of any kind. This book is hard to put down. I recommend it to everyone."
— Mary Erin O'Brien, Author —
Accidental Pilgrim:
From Mammogram to Miracle

Praise

∞

"*Miracles Never Ending* is a wonderful book and an eye opener for Christians, especially charismatics.

Here is my recommendation:

Miracles do happen, as Jesus is ALIVE today.

This book is a revelation of the goodness of our Lord who wants to heal His people. I have known Bro. Bob for the past fifteen years, as he also had prayed for me and my wife and family. I have witnessed myself the healings that people have testified about in this book, which cannot be explained by science. I had the opportunity to accompany Bro. Bob in many of his Healing Rallies, including the one in Thailand, and witnessed physical, emotional, and spiritual healings, including deliverance. I am always amazed at how Jesus reveals Himself through these Healing Rallies.

I have also been impressed with Bro. Bob answering the call of our Lord to do his ministry with such love and dedication, especially at that time when he still held a regular job.

I hope you, too, will discover the love of our Lord to His people through this book."

—Raymundo Caparros, M.D.—
Former Head, Pulmonary Dept.
North Arundel Hospital
(Baltimore-Washington Medical Center)
Glen Burnie, MD

∞

"About one fourth of His time during public ministry was spent by Jesus for healing and delivering people. He has promised that greater things would be possible for those who believe. Therefore, it is not surprising that healings continue to happen and many still experience and witness God's love through healing and deliverance in their life.

I am very happy that Bob Canton has put down his experiences in the healing and deliverance ministry in this beautiful book. The book also teaches us how to pray that miracles do happen. He has also emphasized the need to discern God's will in times of sickness and suffering, as the Lord at times might be wanting us to endure them for our own salvation and for the salvation of others.

Bob has been an active member of the International Catholic Charismatic Renewal Services (ICCRS) Council and has been travelling to different parts of the world for ministry. There have been many testimonies of healing during his ministry. He has a track record of an exemplary life of submission to authorities, love for the Church, commitment to the call, and use of charisms for building up the Body of Christ.

The book is a timely blessing to the Church and the Renewal as it has been written by an experienced leader involved in the ministry of healing. The teachings and testimonies in the book are quite enriching and inspiring. This will help people who are already involved in the ministry and seekers of truth, holiness, and healing. I whole-heartedly recommend the book to everyone hungering for the Word of God and seeking a life in the Spirit."

—Cyril John—
Vice President, ICCRS Council
& Chairman, ICCRS Sub-Committee
for Asia-Oceania

∞

"I met Bob Canton in 1996 in Columbus, Ohio. The following year I joined his pilgrimage group to Israel and Egypt. Five future events prophesied to me in 1992 were fulfilled during this pilgrimage. For five years I kept those words in the silence of my heart. Only afterwards did I reveal the prophetic secrets and soon after, I decided that I would accompany Bob Canton in his ministry. In the eighteen years since, I've been blessed by the Lord to accompany Bob to five continents, including North America, South America, Europe, Australia, Asia, and many other locations multiple times.

The Lord has blessed Bob with a tremendous healing ministry. When you read this book, you will understand the reasons. The Holy Spirit reveals all things to Bob when he is preaching the Gospel or laying on hands in prayer.

I have seen with my eyes multitudes of healings in young and old alike. The blind have been made to see; the deaf have been made to hear. Cysts, lumps, and tumors have disappeared. I've seen the lame made able to walk, and those with canes or walkers put them down, or others walk from their wheelchairs. I've seen people with bone fractures remove their casts because the pain and swelling instantly disappeared. I've seen many deliverances— people delivered from demonic spirits, people who were contaminated from occult practices, rock music, fortune tellers, witchcraft, séances, crystals, voodoo, and so forth. All sorts of body aches and pains, including cancer, heart ailments, asthma, blood disorders, diabetes, and more have been instantly gone away.

For some, only a physician or medical tests can validate the healing. I've heard many times the individual testimonies of certain people who went to the hospital for their respective surgeries, only to find out through additional tests or X-rays that surgery is no longer necessary.

I've heard many testimonies from those who experienced physical, emotional, inner, and spiritual healings. I've heard testimonies by those who were victims or witnesses of violent attacks, rape, or attempted murder.

To me the greatest healing I've seen is the conversion of the heart. When these persons encounter the Risen Jesus in their minds and hearts and become visibly moved by witnessing signs and wonders, sojourners they are being transformed by the Holy Spirit and experiencing Pentecost for the first time.

Many times, non-Christians in Southeast Asia attend the Healing Services out of curiosity only to discover that Jesus is alive. Most of them express a desire to convert to

Praise

Catholicism. 'Come to me, all who labor and are heavy laden, and I will give you rest.'" Matthew 11:28.
—James Leonard Blubaugh—
Mount Vernon, Ohio

"I have known Bob Canton for many years. His book, *Miracles Never Ending,* reflects both his personality and his great faith and trust in a loving God who desires to heal His people. Bob's joy, humility, and transparency endear him to the reader, and opens one up to be challenged and stretched by our God who acts in our day. His testimony of initially strong resistance to the Renewal and the power of the Holy Spirit, even to the point of thinking of 'contact[ing] a lawyer and sue[ing] the church including the people in the prayer group' reminds one of those who have gone before us whose lives were transformed by an encounter with the Lord Jesus Christ, and of their surrender when they ultimately said, 'here I am Lord, I come to do your will.'

May this book open each reader to a deeper experience of the Lord's action to heal, to call, to challenge, and to love us TODAY."
—Walter Matthews—
Executive Director for the National
Service Committee of the Catholic
Charismatic Renewal in the U.S.
Locust Grove, Virginia

Praise

"Getting to know Brother Bob Canton has been one of the biggest blessings in my life. I first met him at one of the healing services he conducted in San Diego, California in the mid 1990s, and from then on we have become the best and closest of friends. I have the great privilege of journeying with him in his ministry to many places in the United States and abroad. In fact, my initiation into the healing ministry took place in Kuching, Malaysia, when Brother Bob invited me to join him together with some friends in a healing crusade he conducted there. That was the first time I ever witnessed the manifestation of evil spirits in many people. But through prayers, many were delivered from demonic oppression and healed of their sicknesses. Some people even converted into the Catholic faith because of the miracles and healings that took place there. But to me, it was a life changing experience as it took my faith and prayer life to a new dimesion.

This book is a veritable testimony to the healing power of the Holy Spirit working through Brother Bob, bringing hope and light to this troubled world and comfort to its suffering people. May the Holy Spirit of God continue to empower Brother Bob in his ministry so that many people will turn to God and become living testimonies to the healing grace of His love."

—Deacon Gus Mora—
St. Joesph the Worker Parish
Winnetka, California

MIRACLES

NEVER ENDING

MIRACLES
NEVER ENDING

*God is Pouring Out His Miraculous Graces
upon His People.
Find Out How You Can Effectively Pray
and Receive Your Miracles.*

Stockton, CA

Robert "Bob" Canton

Publishing consulting and production:

Aimazing Publishing & Marcom, Phoenix, AZ

www.bonniesbooks.com | www.aimazingpmc.com

ISBN # 978-0-692-40223-8

Printed in the USA

First Printing, 2015/Revised January 2016

To my mother Lily Canton,
who first inspired me and encouraged me
to write this book,
and to my wife Chita and my two daughters,
and my entire family who
give their full and unwavering support
for my ministry of preaching, teaching,
and healing,
I dedicate this book.

CONTENTS

Foreword   xxi

Preface   xxv

Encounter with the Divine   1

The Call to Healing Ministry   15

Another Encounter with the Divine   21

Hunger for God   29

Leadership and Miracle Services   35

The Operations of the Gifts   41

Official Launching of the Healing Ministry   53
    by the Lord

Fulfillment of the Prophecy   57

Overview of the Charism of Healing   63
    and Prayer for Healing

How to Pray for Healing and Achieve Results   71

Possible Roadblocks to Healing   83

Can I Be a Miracle Worker?   101

Miraculous Healings of Cancer, Tumors,   111
    and Cysts

Prayer for Healing of Cancer, Tumors, and Cysts   130

Miraculous Healings of Blindness   133
    and Other Eye Diseases

Prayer for Healing of Blindness and Other Eye Diseases   149

Miraculous Healings of Deafness   151
    and Other Ear Diseases

— CONTENTS CONT. —

Prayer for Healing of Deafness and Other Ear Diseases 170
Miraculous Healings of Paralysis   171
   and Other Walking Disabilities
Prayer for Healing of Paralysis   198
   and Other Walking Disabilities
Miraculous Healings of Infertility and Barrenness 201
Prayer for Healing of Infertility and Barrenness   213
Miraculous Healings of the Heart, Lungs,   215
   and Kidneys
Prayer for Healing of the Lungs   233
Prayer for Healing of Heart Diseases   234
Prayer for Healing of Kidney Diseases   235
Miraculous Healings of Various Types of Diseases 237
Prayer for Healing of Various Types of Diseases:
   Healing and Keeping Prayer   267
   Prayer for Empowerment   268
   Spiritual Warfare Prayer   269

—— FOREWORD——

The world is a witness to many and various unexplainable phenomena that are beyond human imagination and intellection. Even science wonders and runs out of reason to elucidate why certain events and incidents happen as these defy logic. While a miracle can be assumed as one of those occurrences where rationality falls short of understanding and even knowing, miracles still happen and it seems they are never ending.

It will be a blessing for many to get to know Bob Canton, a lay person on a special mission preaching and proclaiming God's goodness, power, mercy, and compassion, especially to those who are experiencing physical, spiritual, psychological, and other challenges in their lives. Even though I only came to meet Bob in 2004, we have forged quite a close relationship not only personally but also through our common ministry as followers and disciples of Jesus. It has developed in time as we happened to be together during several Life in the Spirit Seminars, Prayer and Healing Services, and other Charismatic conferences and gatherings. Eventually we become more than dear friends but close partners and collaborators in the mission of evangelization—in preaching the Good News of our salvation in Christ.

Our partnership was galvanized when Bob formed the Alliance of Filipino American Catholic Charismatic

Prayer Communities and requested me to serve as its Episcopal adviser. This provided me many occasions to see and witness the special gift that God has bestowed upon him as an instrument of grace, of healing, of wholeness, and even reconciliation. Through Bob's prayer and invocation of God's Holy Name, people's faith are awakened, their hope restored, their broken spirits mended, and many find their way back to God's loving, healing, and saving embrace.

I find it quite wonderful but humbling to share with Bob the ministry of prayer as well as participate closely in the Church's mission of evangelization. It is amazing to witness the workings of the inspiration of the Holy Spirit and the power of faith in God in the lives of people who seek healing for their sick soul, mind, and body. The words of scriptures come alive again when Christ's grace are revealed and manifested in the miraculous healing that happens right before your eyes and from the confessions or testimonies of the many recipients of such Divine intervention coming from all parts of the world.

His book, *Miracles Never Ending* is an interesting story of Bob's personal account of the various events and incidents through the years of his healing ministry as well as his own perspective and testimonies of those who encountered, received, or experienced God's healing grace. What is impressive in Bob's healing ministry is the preeminence of faith in God who is so rich in mercy, compassion, and kindness. Bob clearly instills the understanding that he is but only a lowly instrument, and it is God who cures, restores, and makes us whole again.

I have no doubt that many will benefit from this book in many ways. It is a source of blessing. Bob helps the people to know, believe, love, and worship God through his own personal encounter with Christ. His faith conviction led him to share the joy of his spiritual experience that others may discover God in their own lives. He exhorts us to expect the unexpected when you believe, when you pray, and when you trust. He teaches that faith opens our lives to many possibilities beyond our imagining and expectations because we have a God of many surprises and our Lord does many wonders. Through prayer, inspiration of the Holy Spirit, and trust in God's power, mercy, and goodness, nothing becomes impossible. Miracles happen. As God continues to exist until the end of time, expect many more surprises because—miracles are never ending.

—Most Reverend Oscar A. Solis, D.D.—
Auxiliary Bishop of Los Angeles, California

While having lunch with my mother Lily to celebrate her birthday with other members of our family back in 2010, my mother commented to me, "Robert, why don't you write a book about those amazing experiences you have had while doing the works for the Lord? I'm sure you have so many materials at your disposal that you can use to write a book, and no doubt many will be blessed by your book."

I told her that many people, in fact, had asked me if I had written a book, especially after I spoke and ministered in conferences and conventions, parish missions, seminars, workshops, and retreats, Healing Rallies and Healing Crusades, and it is somewhat embarrassing for me to always say, "not yet" to them. "So, why don't you write one," was my mother's snappy reply. "Yes, I will ask the Lord Jesus for guidance," was my assurance to her. "I'm sure the Lord will show me the way."

Not long after, my wife and daughters and our close friends had started urging me to write a book. I'd started to believe that the Lord was talking to me through them about writing one. These people were not present, aside from my wife and two daughters, when my mom brought this subject matter up to me. In earnest, I started to pray and to ask direction from the Lord Jesus as to what subject matter to write about.

Preface

"Lord, I want to contribute more, however mundane or insignificant those contributions may be in your sight, to help alleviate the pain and suffering of your people who are sick in body, mind, soul, and spirit. Use me more Lord, in spite of myself, and help me write a book, a book that would help the sick receive your loving, comforting, saving, and healing touch. I know Lord, that you love your people and you want them to be well."

One day, an inspiration and ideas came, coming from the Lord, I'm sure, about writing a book detailing my own conversion experiences and that of my wife's and many members of our family through a visitation from the Holy Trinity that resulted in the Baptism in the Holy Spirit. The Baptism in the Holy Spirit is an experience of the presence and power and love of God that transforms a person and makes him a new person inside. Furthermore, many ideas came pouring into my mind as to the contents of the book: the teachings on how to effectively pray for the sick, how to avoid the blockages to healing, how to receive and use the gifts of the Holy Spirit in healing the sick, what are the teachings of the Roman Catholic Church regarding healing, the scripture passages about Jesus and His apostles and disciples healing the sick, and the use of various testimonies of people who have been healed in Jesus' Name through the power of the Holy Spirit. Then I heard the Lord speaking into my heart," My son, I want you to write specific healing prayers for some specific illnesses, and I will supply the words to you. I will anoint these prayers to heal in my Name for the glory and honor of the Holy Trinity."

Preface

I started writing this book in late 2010, but because of the demands of constant traveling and ministering throughout the world, I was not able to finish it until after Thanksgiving Day in 2014. I managed to write fourteen chapters in a period of less than three weeks. Of course, I was able to do this through the help and inspiration of the Holy Spirit! Blessed be His Name forever!

I cannot thank the Lord enough for the graces that He is bestowing upon me. It is my fervent prayer and hope, and I firmly believe, that His people will experience miracles through reading this book and by using the healing prayers contained herein, not because of me and what I wrote, but because of who He is and how awesome and powerful and loving He is. After all, "for God nothing is impossible at all." (cf. Luke 1:37). Indeed, our God is a miracle working God. The Lord is always true and faithful to His promises. For all of these, I am thanking Him from the core of my being.

I also would like to thank everyone who helped me and inspired me tremendously in writing this book: My late mother Lily, my wife and daughters, all my family members and friends, especially the members of the Children of God Prayer Community of St. Luke's Parish in Stockton, California, notably the intercessory, music, and healing ministries. I thank Bishop Oscar Solis, Auxiliary Bishop for the Archdiocese of Los Angeles, who wrote the foreword for this book, Fr. Ramon Zarate, the current pastor of St. Luke's Parish, Fr. Joe Maghinay, parochial vicar of the Presentation Parish in Stockton, who is my spiritual adviser, Michelle Moran, ICCRS President, Cyril John, ICCRS Vice President, Patti and Al Mansfield, Liaisons for the Charismatic Renewal in the Archdiocese of New Orleans, Walter Matthews, Executive Director for the National Service Committee of the Catholic Charismatic Renewal in the U.S., Mary Erin O'Brien, Author, Sally Ann Quinones, Author, and Dr. Al Albarracin and Dr. Ray Caparros who wrote endorsements for this book.

I also thank my brother Nilo, my friends James Blubaugh and Al Pineda, Deacon Gus and Onie Mora, Deacon Leo and Fe Lacbain, Dr. Jose and Agnes Nepomuceno, Dr. Anastacio and Dey Pinzon, and Marico and Fe Enriquez, who have accompanied me multiple times in many parts of the world, all those who sent me their testimonies of healings and miracles and restorations for God's glory, and Joe Ciezenski who encouraged me "unceasingly" in writing this book, as well as the countless people here and abroad who have been praying for me and my family and for my ministry. Last but not least, I thank Bonnie Crutcher who did all the work (consulting, copy editing, typesetting, designing, coordinating the printing) and all the preparations to make this book ready for printing and publication.

But most of all, I would like to thank the Lord Jesus because "with and through Him, we can do all things." (cf. Phil. 4:13) "For in Him we live and move and have our being." (Acts 17:28)

To God be the glory for ever, and ever, Amen!

CHAPTER ONE

Encounter with the Divine

On Saturday, November 11, 1984, my wife Chita and I received the Baptism in the Holy Spirit during a Growth in the Spirit Seminar at the Church of the Presentation Parish in Stockton, California. The Baptism in the Holy Spirit or Personal Pentecost is an experience of the presence of the living God and the power of His Holy Spirit. According to the document of the Baptism in the Holy Spirit, which was prepared and issued by the Doctrinal Commission of the Vatican-based International Catholic Charismatic Renewal Services (ICCRS),

> Baptism in the Spirit is an experience of the love of God the Father poured into one's heart, leading to a transformed life in the lordship of Jesus and the power of the Holy Spirit. This grace brings alive sacramental

baptism and confirmation, enkindling evangelistic fervor and equipping a person with charisms for service and mission.

"...this seminar was something different than the 'ordinary experiences' with God."

It was one of the most significant and dramatic experiences, if not the most significant and dramatic experience, Chita and I have ever had in our lives with the living God.

My cousin, Avelina, who had been actively involved in the Catholic Charismatic Renewal while she was still residing in the Philippines, strongly urged my wife and me to attend the Life in the Spirit Seminar that was held in the Presentation Parish in September 1984. At the time, we gave her many excuses not to attend the seminar, telling her that we pray and we go to Sunday Mass anyway. We didn't feel that we needed to go to this seminar. Two months later, a Growth in the Spirit seminar was scheduled in the same venue. The seminar was scheduled for Friday evening, November 10, until Sunday afternoon, November 12. That time, Avelina was more persuasive than before, telling us that this seminar was something different than the "ordinary experiences" with God. She promised us that we would like it. At first, we argued with her that since we missed the basic seminar, it was not right for us to go to the Growth in the Spirit seminar. She said it didn't really matter at all. "Besides," she assured us, "nobody would notice anyway." We came up with so many excuses under the sun why we could not attend the seminar. However, my cousin was very persistent.

Finally, to please her, and since she was babysitting our daughter, my wife and I decided to attend the seminar on Saturday morning for an hour only. My wife was planning to go shopping that day anyway. Our plan was to leave quietly when nobody was looking and go straight to the shopping mall. We did not attend the Friday evening session.

On Saturday morning, as we were about to leave the house, the automatic garage door opener broke, and Chita and I argued in the car on the way to the Presentation Parish gym where the seminar was being held. We arrived late as a result. As we listened to the talks and testimony given by a husband and wife, Elena and Jess Molina, I felt like my heart was burning because they were speaking from their hearts, and I could somehow relate to what they were talking about. Next, another couple gave their testimony on how the Lord Jesus had saved their floundering marriage. I was very moved; so was Chita. Subsequently, Chita and I decided to stay for the whole day. My two sisters-in-law, Carmen and Luz Canton, were also present with us.

During lunch, the four of us shared with one another about how we were deeply touched by the sincerity of the speakers and the powerful talks they gave. A married couple, Mary and Julian Sepulveda and Deacon Bill Brennan of the Presentation Parish, the prayer group leader and the Episcopal Liaison for the Catholic Charismatic Renewal for the Diocese of Stockton, and now a retired professor of Russian History at the University of the Pacific, gave talks and testimonies in the afternoon until early evening. Afterward, during the Mass that followed, we heard some people singing in a strange language, which we learned later on was "praising and singing in tongues."

Resting (Slain) In the Spirit

After Communion, a leader of our seminar's sharing group, Lilian Martinez, went down on the floor as if she "fainted." To my horror, nobody came to her rescue. I whispered to Chita, who is a registered nurse, to give her first aid. As Chita walked toward Lilian, someone stopped her and advised her not to touch Lilian. I thought to myself, *What kind of people are these? What if Lilian had a heart attack and nobody is doing anything to revive her? And they even stopped my wife from giving her first aid!* I was very much disturbed, to say the least, by the group's apparent "inaction" and seeming lack of concern to what happened to Lilian. A few minutes later, Lilian stood up and seemed to be fine. Despite my feelings of frustration, I was greatly relieved that she was alright. Later on, I found out that Lilian experienced a phenomenon called 'resting in the Spirit' or 'slain in the Spirit' or 'dormition.' It is a phenomenon wherein the Holy Spirit touches our human spirit, and we sense a feeling of physical weakness and we fall down backwards. However, we don't lose consciousness or control of our body. A person who experiences this phenomenon is generally very much aware of their surroundings. They usually sense a feeling of peace and a feeling of being "at rest" in God's presence.

After the priest gave his blessing at the conclusion of the Mass, Deacon Bill Brennan asked the group to form a big circle inside the Parish gym. Then he asked the group to close their eyes, and he recited some prayers. Next, the group began singing until it seemed like everybody except the four of us, Chita, me, Carmen, and Luz, were once again praising and singing in tongues. Their eyes were closed but somehow they sang in tongues in synchronous intervals. It seemed like they started doing it at the same time and they also stopped at the same time. I started to wonder if we had gotten caught in the middle of a cultist activity. Some feelings of anguish and fear came into my heart. I kept my eyes opened and I tried to observe everything that was going on around us. And then someone spoke out loud, saying, "I am Jesus and don't be afraid because I am with you." I was convinced; *No doubt—this group is cultist. Someone is even pretending to be Jesus,* I thought to myself. I didn't realize that person had given a prophecy or a message from God. (The gift of prophecy is mentioned in 1 Corinthians 12 and 1 Corinthians 14).

After this message, Deacon Brennan and some leaders of the prayer group started to lay hands on the people, and everyone that they touched went down on the floor. When this started happening, I felt I had to leave and told Chita that it was time to go. But we were bound by our hands being held and were locked in to each other in the circle. I was standing next to a tall gentleman named Ed, a burly gentleman who was probably around six feet tall, singing his heart out with his eyes closed while holding my hands tightly. The more I tried to pull my hand out of his grasp, the tighter he was grasping it. I felt like we were arm wrestling with each other and finally I gave up because he didn't want to let go of my hand. He had his eyes closed all the time. *These men are hypnotizing these people, but I will fight any power that they may have by looking directly at their eyes when they lay hands on me. No way am I falling down on the floor,* I thought to myself. Suddenly, a few minutes later, my legs buckled; I went down on the floor, and my mouth started to babble. *Oh, oh, I'm infected by this cultish group,* I said to myself. I felt so embarrassed that I went down on the floor and no one was even touching me. Deacon Brennan and the other leaders were still a few feet away from me. Because of this embarrassment, I wanted to get up right away, but my legs felt like rubber bands. My legs lost their strength and I couldn't get up right away, no matter how hard I tried. This strange event lasted a few minutes. While on the floor, I wondered why this man Ed finally let go of me. He didn't even attempt to hold me back as I was going down.

He is not very nice, after all, I thought to myself. When I was finally able to get up, I saw Chita still standing. But a few minutes later, she went down on the floor together with Luz, and then Car-

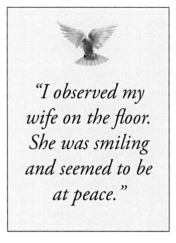

"I observed my wife on the floor. She was smiling and seemed to be at peace."

men followed them on the floor. Deacon Brennan and other leaders of the group were still a few feet away from them as well. Chita stayed on the floor for a long time. When I realized forty minutes had passed and she was still on the floor, I put her on a chair, but minutes later she slid back down to the floor with a smile on her face. An hour had passed, and then two hours. She was still on the floor. Finally, everybody had left except Deacon Brennan and some of the prayer leaders of the Presentation Parish prayer group. Chita was still on the floor being ministered to by the prayer leaders. A lady named Judy asked me if there was something that happened to my wife that was traumatic. I told her that she lost her father two years earlier and her brother died of a motorcycle accident a few months after she had lost her dad. Judy said that the Holy Spirit was healing Chita emotionally. I observed my wife on the floor. She was smiling and seemed to be at peace. Deep inside me, I was angry, scared, and perplexed. My wife was smiling while I was worrying about her. Nobody seemed to give a good explanation as to what was happening to us. Three hours had passed. She was still on the floor. Finally, I decided to go home. I asked two other people to help me walk her to the car. She looked as if she was drunk and she could hardly walk. (Actually, she was drunk in the Holy Spirit as we learned later on.) I decided to put Chita in the back seat of the car. Luz volunteered to sit next to her. I thought Chita had "too much of it." All kinds of thoughts went through my mind: *What if she stays like this, God forbid; what will happen to us? If our neighbors would see us, they would probably say that we just came back from a bar or party where alcohol was served.*

As I drove off, Chita started to speak in tongues. Minutes later, Luz did the same. It seemed like they had a contest as to who could speak faster and longer. It seemed like they were having conversations with each other. I did not know what to do. This was too much for me to handle. A barrage of thoughts wrangled my mind. *Should I go back to the Presentation gym, or should I take them somewhere? But where? For sure, everybody had already left Presentation gym. If this continues, and something happens, God forbid, I will contact a lawyer and sue the church including the people in the prayer group at Presentation parish.* I blamed those people for what happened to Chita and Luz. Nevertheless, I decided to go straight home. I was doing 15 MPH in a 35 MPH zone, but it seemed like Chita and Luz were having conversations in tongues "much faster than I was driving." On the way home, I was also blaming my cousin, Avelina, for convincing us to attend the seminar. As a matter of fact I was very mad at her for doing so.

A Stunning, Personal Message from God

As soon as we arrived home, I had to walk Chita and Luz from the car. I was holding Chita with my right hand and Luz with my left because they could hardly walk. My cousin, Avelina, opened the door leading to the garage, and as soon as she saw us, she exclaimed, "Praise the Lord. How beautiful! They received the Baptism in the Holy Spirit." As soon as she said it, I raised my voice at her in anger, "Look what happened. It is because of you and that cultist group. It is really a very strange group of people." She said, "Calm down. The Holy Spirit really touched them. Wow." But I just ignored her. Then Chita and Luz walked around inside the house with their eyes closed. They kept on saying, "The Lord is my Shepherd, I shall not want," over and over again. They seemed to know where they were going. They never bumped into each other or into a chair or a table or any furniture or any object inside the house. I made a comment to my cousin, "What are they saying? Isn't that a prayer that a priest says during a funeral service? Why do they keep on saying it?" She answered, "Just listen and pay attention. It is in Psalm 23. I believe that the Lord is saying

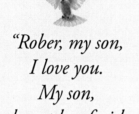

*"Rober, my son,
I love you.
My son,
do not be afraid.
My name is Jesus.
I'm here
to visit you. "*

to us that we are in His presence and under His protection." Then Chita came to me with her eyes closed, saying, "Rober, my son, I love you. My son, do not be afraid. My name is Jesus. I'm here to visit you." With fright, I walked away and stayed as far away from her as possible. I turned to my cousin and asked her, "Why is she calling me Rober? She is calling me her son also. I'm her husband, not her son! (By the way, my baptized name is Roberto.) Now she is thinking that she is my mother. She also says she is Jesus! I'm sure she was contaminated by those cultist people in the church." "That is what we call prophecy or a message from God," my cousin Avelina tried to explain.

I raised my voice at her a little bit in frustration and anger, "I don't care what it is. I think it's very, very strange." By this time I decided to call my parents to ask them to come to my house. My mother Lily answered the phone call. I told her that Chita and Luz needed help—bad. She asked what happened, and I told her they were acting really "weird." I told her that it was hard to explain but that she would find out when she came to the house.

A 'Word of Knowledge" Revealed to My Father

My parents must have sensed the urgency to come right away because ten minutes later, my father Petronilo and my mom arrived. As soon as they entered my house, Chita and Luz approached them at the door. Their eyes were closed all this time. Chita told them, "My children, thank you for coming, I love you my children. Come in. My name is Jesus," and Luz and Chita were saying something in tongues. It's hard to describe my parents' facial expressions. I could only say that they were frightened and very much perplexed just like me, to say the least. Then my father turned to me and asked me, "Where have you been?" "To church," I told him.

Then Chita came to my father and said to him, "My son Petronilo, I love you, my son. You had pain here, and here, and here," while touching his shoulder, his back, and his neck, "but I'm healing you, my son. Do not be afraid. My name is Jesus. I'm using your daughter-in-law to heal you." Then she was praying something in tongues while laying her hands on the affected parts of my father's body. The eyes of my father became bigger. He said, "How does she know all the pains in my body? She is exactly right." I just shrugged my shoulders. Then my cousin said, "Don't worry, Papa, God is healing you." Then Chita said, "My son, this is what happened to you when you were seventeen years of age to make you believe that I'm speaking to you." Then she proceeded to tell him what happened to him.

My father commented to me that he was the only one who knew about it and nobody else. He didn't even tell my mom nor anybody else in the family about what happened to him. He was so amazed that Chita knew about it. My cousin told him that it was the Holy Spirit who told Chita about it through prophecy and 'word of knowledge.' I could not really fathom or understand what my cousin was telling us. My father then turned to me and told me in a soft voice that the pains in his body disappeared instantly after Chita prayed over him.

I decided to call my brother Leo, Luz's husband, and asked him to come to my house. I told him in a hurried way what had been happening to Luz and Chita inside the house. I could tell that he was angry. He said that he tried to persuade Luz not to attend the seminar because he had heard that charismatics are "weird and crazy people," but Luz did not listen to him and decided to attend anyway. When he came into the house ten minutes later, he started to rant and he was visibly upset. While still at the door, Leo started blaming Luz for what happened to her. Luz stood squarely in front of Leo about ten feet away from him, extending both hands towards him with her eyes still closed, praying in tongues. Leo suddenly went down on the floor and he stayed there for some time. *Oh, oh, I have another problem here,* I thought to myself. Luz and Chita said many things that night and quoted scriptures. They kept on saying these words, "I love you, all my children. Do not be afraid, because I am with you. My mother Mary is with you. The angels are with you. My Father is blessing all of you." At about 2:00 A.M., both Chita and Luz went down on the floor for about ten to fifteen minutes. Afterwards, they related to us what happened to them while they were under the 'anointing' of the Holy Spirit. Chita said that she was surrounded with a loving presence, a loving embrace of what she sensed as God the Father. Luz said she was in the mighty presence of the Lord. They shared with us their visions of God the Father, Jesus, Mary, angels, and saints. They claimed they were walking on "streets of gold." They told us that they only repeated the words that they heard from their 'inner being,' directly from the Lord. They said that they saw a very bright light the entire time it had been going on. There was a sense of peace and calm and serenity inside the house. We could actually feel the presence of God among us. My parents and I and Leo were very much relieved after we heard this explanation from them. Leo told us that when Luz extended her hands towards him, he felt a powerful but "gentle" force, which brought him down. He said he could never forget that experience. My father Petronilo said that it was the first time for him ever to experience God in a very powerful way. On my part, I would liken it to a loving, gentle "tornado" that touched us, if there ever was such a term. Luz, Leo, my cousin Avelina, my parents, Chita, and I then prayed the Rosary in the early hours of November 12, 1984.

That experience with the Divine is still very fresh in my mind, as if it just happened a few hours ago. It was an experience that started a radical change in our lives, a change that is still going on—a spiritual rebirth—a change that we hope and pray will continue.

CHAPTER TWO

The Call
to Healing Ministry

O
n that day, November 11, 1984, Chita and
Luz received myriad spiritual gifts instantly,
such as the gifts of tongues, prophecy, word
of knowledge, word of wisdom, and healing among
other gifts, including the gift of vision. The manifestations of these gifts of the Holy Spirit through them
were ubiquitous that very day and more so in the succeeding days, weeks, months, and years that followed.
It had so impacted our lives that we started to pray
together as husband and wife and as a family after this
powerful experience with the Lord Jesus. It was during one of these prayer gatherings that my parents and
many of my relatives received the Baptism in the Holy
Spirit that also changed their lives in a very powerful
way. I bought the very first Bible that I ever had owned

in my life. Chita did the same thing. We started reading the Bible, and we could not put it down. For the first time in our lives we realized how hungry we were for the word of God. We felt that we could not get enough of His words. We read and read and read the Bible until the wee hours of the morning.

"You Will Travel Far and Wide"

Almost a month later, on December 8, 1984, on the Feast of the Immaculate Conception, Chita and I were praying the Rosary together in our room at around 8:00 P.M. She fell down on the floor, 'resting' in the Holy Spirit and praying in tongues. After a few minutes, she stood up and picked up the Bible from the table, and with both of her eyes closed and praying in tongues, started to leaf through the Bible in a very rapid fashion. Then, with both eyes still closed, she opened the Bible and pointed to Chapter 6 of the book of the prophet Isaiah, saying, "My son, Rober, I want you to read this."

After I finished reading the entire chapter, I put it on the table. Then Chita picked it up again; still with her eyes closed, she leafed through the Bible in a more rapid fashion than the first time and, with her eyes closed, opened it to Isaiah 6, saying to me, "Rober, my son, I want you to read this slowly and carefully." This time, I was really amazed and I started to wonder how she was able to do what she did with her eyes closed.

I closed the Bible and put it back again on the table after I read the passage. "My son, I want you to really read it very slowly and carefully, and I want you to put these words into your heart." For the third time Chita repeated what she did with her eyes still closed. As I was reading this chapter, I felt that my heart was pierced with the words starting on verses 5-10, "Then I said, 'Woe is me, I am doomed! For I am a man of unclean lips, living among a people of unclean lips; yet my eyes have seen the King, the Lord of Host!' Then one of the seraphim flew to me, holding an ember, which he had taken with tongs from the altar. He touched my mouth with it. 'See,' he said, 'now that this has touched your lips, your wickedness is removed, your sin purged.' Then I heard the voice of the Lord saying, 'Whom shall I send? Who will go for us?' 'Here I am,' I said: 'send me!'"

After I finished reading, Chita turned to me, saying, "I love you my son. My son, Rober, I'm talking to you through my daughter, through your wife. My name is Jesus. Do not be afraid. I am going to use you to heal millions in my Name, because healing is good news. If anyone needs healing, then heal in my Name. Be humble always my son. You will preach the good news, the Gospel, in my Name. You will travel far and wide; you will set foot on places that you have not even dreamed of seeing. You set the limits as to where you want to go. Pray always. Do not be afraid, for I am with you. You find it hard to believe, but it will come to pass, my son." I was incredulous when I heard those words. I said to myself, *heal millions? What does it mean? Preaching the Gospel? No way, I am not a priest nor a deacon.*

Besides, I don't know how to preach the Gospel in front of people. No, not me. Going places? I don't have any extra money to go to far away places just to preach the good news. Besides, I am the wrong person to do these things because I am a sinner. My wife is probably just imagining things. For sure, she has the wrong person here," I thought to myself. After she had prophesied, she touched the top of my head and started praying in tongues. I felt the powerful and wonderful presence of the Lord Jesus. Then I started to shake and shake and shake. I felt so small; I felt my "nothingness" in the presence of the Lord. I felt like I was in a different realm, in the realm of God's presence and power, in the realm of His love.

"... God doesn't usually call those who are qualified but He qualifies those He calls,..."

Then I fell down on the floor and "rested in the spirit." Then she said, "My son, I want you and my daughter to go to Confession together as soon as possible. Do not delay. I want you to receive my Sacrament of Reconciliation. I want you to have a pure and clean heart." I had not been to Confession for more than two years. Two days later, Chita and I went to Confession at St. Mary's Church in downtown Stockton. When it was over, I felt as though something heavy had been lifted from me. I felt so free, so light. I felt so close to the Lord and I felt this overwhelming and indescribable joy in my heart. I felt like the Lord Jesus was really walking with me in flesh and blood. I felt so secure and safe for the first time in my life. I related this experience with a close friend of mine not long afterwards. I told her that I found it hard to believe that the Lord would ever use me because I felt like I was the worst sinner in the entire world. My friend said, "Bob, if the Lord can use a donkey, there is no reason why He cannot use you." "Thank you for boosting up my confidence," I told her with a giggle. "I heard somebody say that God doesn't usually call those who are qualified but He qualifies those whom He calls," she recalled.

I also told my friend that Chita and Luz call me the name Rober every time that they are anointed to deliver a message for me from the Lord. "Bob, the Lord calls you that name because that is your name in Heaven. Do you realize that? As a matter of fact, it is in Exodus 33:12. God says, "I know you by name and you have also found favor in my sight," my friend told me with obvious excitement on her face. A feeling of exhilaration was also bubbling within me, because I realized that the Lord had revealed to me my true name in Heaven!

I thank and praise the Lord of the Harvest for opening doors over the years and allowing me to minister to fifty countries so far all over the world.

Meeting His Holiness Pope Francis in 2014 outside St. Peter's Basilica in the Vatican

CHAPTER THREE

Another Encounter with the Divine

O ne morning, a few weeks after I received the prophecy, I was wide-awake. I felt like the Lord Jesus was talking to me and I heard His voice in my heart. He said, "My son, I want you to kneel down and pray." I looked at my watch. It was 2:00 A.M. I said to myself, *it's too early to pray, and I have to get up early to go to work.*

The following day, the same thing happened. I was again wide-awake at 2:00 A.M. and I heard the same words in my heart. I had the same excuse and went right back to sleep. I related this to Chita, who said to me, "Why did you ignore the Lord? If I were you, I would do what He tells me to do." I told her that if it were to happen again, I would certainly do it. I was hoping that if He would wake me up that early again,

He would do it either on a Saturday or Sunday morning, because I did not have to go to work on weekends.

Photographic Visions

The following morning, which was a Saturday, I was awake at exactly 2:00 A.M. I heard the same words in my heart that I had received the previous two days. In addition, I also heard these words, "My son, humble yourself before me and worship me with all of your heart." I went downstairs and I knelt before the picture of the Sacred Heart of Jesus, which is on the fireplace mantle. I started to sing praise songs and worshipped Him. Suddenly, I saw a "vision" or a "mental picture" which was as clear as day. The vision was of the Lord Jesus, wearing a white robe, standing before multitudes of people in an open, wide field. I was a few feet behind him, and He was motioning to me to come and stand next to Him. He said, "Rober, come, my son, and extend your hands to them." I said, Lord, please not me. I am not worthy to do it. He said, "My son, I died for you on the Cross in order for you to become worthy of me. Do not be afraid. Remember I am with you. Come, my son, they are waiting for me, and they are waiting for you." Slowly and reluctantly, I walked towards the Lord and I stood next to Him as He asked me to do. As He raised His hands toward the people, I followed Him. I saw the people falling down on the ground. The succeeding visions seemed like I was viewing them on photographic slides. I saw myself sitting next to the Lord in a jet plane, in a car, in a gigantic ship, and in a small boat. The Lord and I were walking alongside a freeway. I didn't know what these visions meant then. With my hands lifted up, I kept on thanking and praising the Lord Jesus. Suddenly, I felt like my hands were on fire. I saw in a vision something like "liquid crystals" touching

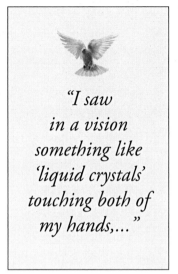

"I saw in a vision something like 'liquid crystals' touching both of my hands,..."

both of my hands, like electric currents going through my hands. I felt like my hands were on fire! Minutes later, I fell face down, and I could not move. It seemed like my body was glued to the ground, yet it felt like my body was as light as a feather, as if I was floating on air. I could not explain or describe fully how I felt. I thought I was on the floor for 10-20 minutes. Time flew so fast, it seemed. But actually I had stayed in this position for almost three hours, basking in God's presence and glory.

I would like to state here that those "photographic visions" that I had have already come into reality. The visions where I found myself sitting next to the Lord on a jet plane, and where the Lord and I were in a car are self-explanatory. During our third pilgrimage to the Holy Land in 1998, one of our scheduled activities was a cruise on the Sea of Galilee. When the day came for this cruise to take place, it was a very stormy and windy day. It even snowed in Jerusalem, which was a very rare occurrence. Out of the thirty-eight pilgrims in our group, only twenty-two of us decided to go on this cruise. Even though I had taken this cruise twice before, I had to be with these twenty-one pilgrims, being the tour leader. While waiting for the boat from the pier, we noticed that the small boat, on the way to pick us up, was dancing on the waves, and the waves were breaking over the boat. The boat operators had a hard time docking it on the pier. Finally, we had to literally jump into the boat from the docking platform. As soon as everybody was on board, Fr. Harmon Skillin, the pastor of St. Luke's Parish in Stockton, and who at that time was our pilgrimage's spiritual adviser, led the prayers of thanksgiving and protection. Afterwards, he led the group in singing, "Michael Row the Boat Ashore."

At this juncture, the wind seemed to be getting stronger and stronger, and some of our fellow pilgrims were starting to get worried and scared. So, I stationed myself on the starboard side of the boat towards the front so that I could use the microphone. "My fellow pilgrims, don't you realize that the Lord is allowing us to experience a violent storm in the Sea of Galilee?" I asked. Then I quoted to them from the book of Matthew 8:23-27.

> He got into a boat and his disciples followed
> him. Suddenly a violent storm came up on

> the sea, so that the boat was being swamped by waves; but he was asleep. They came and woke him, saying, "Lord, save us! We are perishing!" He said to them, "Why are you terrified, O you of little faith? Then he got up, rebuked the winds and the sea, and there was great calm. The men were amazed and said, "What sort of man is this, whom even the winds and the sea obey?

I then assured my fellow pilgrims, "I believe this is a blessing for us from the Lord, so that we can see and experience His glory again today." I then encouraged them to join me in commanding the storm to quiet down and the wind to stop in the mighty Name of Jesus. "There is power in the Name of Jesus, so let us say it with faith," I exhorted them. Everyone, in unison, began commanding the wind and the waves to calm down.

Halfway through our cruise on the way to the shore of Tiberias, the rain and the wind had stopped completely, and the waves had calmed down. The dark clouds had dissipated, and the sun came out. Everybody was dancing and praising the Lord in the boat, in total awe of what the Lord had done for us. Then I asked the operators of the boat to turn off the engine. We all sat still for at least ten minutes so that we could only hear the soft rushing of the waves on the boat and the chirping of the birds that were hovering over us. Everybody was enveloped with total peace and calmness and with

> *"My son, Rober, I am here with all of you in this boat," the Lord spoke into my heart. "Fear no more, because you are all safe in my hands."*

the presence of the Lord. A gentle sea breeze came to "caress" everyone. "My son, Rober, I am here with all of you in this boat," the Lord spoke into my heart. "Fear no more, because you are all safe in my hands."

Back in 2002, while I was driving on Interstate 5 from Stockton to conduct a seminar on Spiritual Gifts and a Healing Rally in San Francisco, my car broke down. I had to walk alongside the freeway to find a telephone box for me to use to call for help. Without a doubt, the Lord was there with me. The help came right away, and I arrived in San Francisco just in time for the start of the seminar and the Healing Rally.

The vision of the Lord and I in a gigantic ship was fulfilled in 2003, when my wife and I and fifty-eight other people in our group, including ten of Chita's former classmates from college and their respective spouses, went on a seven-day Mexican Riviera cruise, departing from Los Angeles, California, aboard the Norwegian Star of the Norwegian Cruise Line, which has a total capacity of 2,348 passengers. While on board, Deacon Bill Brennan and I conducted a Life in the Spirit Seminar. We conducted the seminar in a bar room of the cruise ship because that was the only room available for us.

We held the seminar during the day when the bar service was not available. Many people in our group received the Baptism in the Holy Spirit and many of them got drunk in the Holy Spirit, literally. The name of the room was, "The Wheel Bar." The Holy Spirit really has a sense of humor!

This experience of the Baptism in the Holy Spirit has changed the lives of those who were there upside down and inside out. To this day, they have their own respective ministries in the Roman Catholic Church, and two of our closest friends have been ordained Deacons of the Church.

In 2004, we embarked on a seven-day Inside Passage Alaskan cruise, departing from Seattle, Washington, aboard the Norwegian Cruise Line's Star of the Sea. We also held a Life In the Spirit Seminar aboard that ship. The Lord touched many people at that seminar, and healings also took place.

Part of the attendees during the Healing Crusade in Pontianak, Borneo, Indonesia

Ministering during a Healing Crusade in Pontianak, Borneo, Indonesia

CHAPTER FOUR

Hunger for God

S ince that celestial and glorious experience, which
I believe had been another visitation of the Lord
Jesus through the power of the Holy Spirit, my
hunger for the Lord had intensified to a degree that I
had never imagined possible. I started to go to Mass
and received Holy Communion daily. His words in
scriptures were like music to my ears and give comfort
to my heart. This is a big departure from my attitude in
the past when I used to dislike priests who gave more
than ten minutes of homily during Mass. Now I cling
to every word that the priest says during homily, and I
feel a little bit dissatisfied when the priest only gives a
very short sermon. I started to talk about the Lord and
my experiences with Him to my relatives, friends, and
acquaintances, and to my co-workers in ways I never

expected to be possible before. I felt like a different person inside. I used to be very anxious about many things in life, but this time I really felt liberated from anxieties and worries. I felt so free and joyful. I just could not get enough of the Lord and His words.

Soon, my wife and I started to attend a prayer meeting once a week at the Church of the Presentation. My family members, including my cousins and in-laws, had started to pray together either at my house or at Luz and Leo's residence, or at my parents' home more than twice a week (and in many instances four times a week). During these prayer sessions with my close relatives, we received words of prophecies and words of knowledge and wisdom and words of empowerment from Luz and Chita. Healings also took place. In one of the prayer sessions, a directive came from the Lord through words of prophecy to write down all the messages that were given to us by the Holy Spirit. I constantly longed for my family to get together and pray together. It didn't matter to us that most of the time these prayer sessions lasted for three to four hours when we came together to pray. Every time we received some messages, I made it a point to read them to Fr. Sebastian Drake, OFM, a priest who was involved in the Catholic Charismatic Renewal and a former official exorcist for the Diocese of Stockton, and to Deacon Bill Brennan, for discernment. Both of them told me that in these messages, they could not find anything objectionable or anything contrary to the teachings of the Roman Catholic Church.

Fr. Sebastian told me, "Bob, do you realize that what has been happening to you and to your family is a visitation from the Lord? What a tremendous blessing from the Lord to you and to your family." What he told me gave joy and excitement and encouragement to my heart. He gave confirmations and assurance that what had been hap-

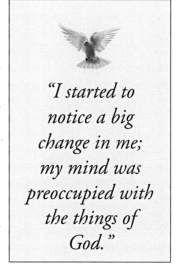

"I started to notice a big change in me; my mind was preoccupied with the things of God."

pening to us since November 11, 1984, was from God, pure and simple.

My hunger for the Lord and His words was so intense that I started to read books about the Holy Trinity, the gifts of the Holy Spirit, the lives of the saints, and other religious books aside from the Bible. I started to notice a big change in me; my mind was preoccupied with the things of God. I could not get enough of Him and I loved to talk about the Lord and my experiences with God to those who were willing to listen. As I said earlier in this book, some of my anxieties about the vagaries of life in general had vanished and they had been replaced with excitement and great expectations of the goodness and kindness of the Lord. I could hardly wait to wake up the following day because I truly felt that the Lord would show and reveal to me new things each and every day. I started to really feel a zest for life—that life is worth living, because the Lord is for us and with us, according to God's words in Deuteronomy 31:6,

> Be strong and steadfast; have no fear or dread of them, for it is the LORD, your God, who marches with you; he will never fail you or forsake you.

I became full of hope, joy, and peace. Moreover, my attitudes towards people and things around me changed a lot for the better. In other words, slowly but surely, I had become a new person inside. In 2 Corinthians 5:17, St. Paul said,

> If anyone is in Christ, he becomes a new creation. Everything is new. The old has passed away.

For sure, all these changes in me had been brought about through the pure grace of God alone, and not by my own doing or my own being. My constant prayer is for this conversion process to go on throughout my entire life. I have not arrived as of yet. I still have a long way to go. But one thing is sure. I am not the same person that I used to be. Glory be to God!

Meanwhile, I longed to receive spiritual gifts from the Lord, especially the gifts of tongues and prophecy. One day while I was praying, I asked the Lord, "Why is it that you only gave these spiritual gifts to my wife and not me?" Somehow, I heard the Lord speaking into my heart. He said, "I have given you the gifts, my son, and I want you to use them with faith and humility. Open up your heart wide to me. I want you to use your gifts for my glory." Not long afterwards, I was attending Mass one Sunday morning at St. Luke's Parish by myself because Chita and my family were spending the weekend with my sister-in-law in the Bay area. While the priest was invoking the Holy Spirit to bless the bread and the wine prior to his reciting the prayer for consecration, or epiclesis, my mouth started to babble in a "strange language" or tongues. The person to my right and to my left heard the "tongues," and they turned to me and asked, "Are you alright?" "Yes, I am, thank you," I said to them. On the way home from church, I was praying in tongues with great enthusiasm, excitement and, yes, with "gusto."

I felt like dancing and singing at the same time. Every day since then, as I pray and sing in tongues, I sense that the Holy Spirit keeps on adding more words into this prayer language.

In Romans 8:26-27, St. Paul said,

> In the same way, the Spirit too comes to the aid of our weakness; for we do not know how to pray as we ought, but the Spirit itself intercedes with inexpressible groanings. And the one who searches hearts knows what is the intention of the Spirit, because it intercedes for the holy ones according to God's will.

It is really a faith-building experience to have this gift in operation in your life. As St. Paul said, in 1 Corinthians 14:2,

> For one who speaks in a tongue does not speak to human beings but to God, for no one listens; he utters mysteries in spirit.

This gift of praying in tongues has helped my prayer life tremendously. And it still does.

CHAPTER FIVE

Leadership and Miracle Services

In March 1985, the door opened for me to become a prayer group leader for an existing prayer group at St. Luke's Parish. A distant relative of mine, Steve Enad, called me one day in March to say that he was going to relocate to Washington, D.C. He said that he was leading a prayer group at St. Luke's Parish and that he and his wife Tessie had been praying and asking the Lord as to who would take their place as prayer group leaders. He said that my name and my face came up while they were praying and trying to discern the Lord's direction for them. He told me that the Lord wanted me to lead the group. I told him that I wasn't ready and that I felt inadequate to lead a group whose members I didn't even know and I hadn't even met yet. Besides, I didn't know how to lead a prayer group.

I told him that my wife and I just started attending prayer meetings at Presentation parish and reading the Bible. I flatly said, "No" to him. I told him that I didn't want to take the role of "a blind man leading the blind." I told him further that I didn't want to be the "laughing stock" of people in the group. He told me to pray about it. He kept on calling me everyday for four days, trying to convince me to say "Yes" to the Lord, according to him. Steve must have been very desperate to find a replacement for him and his wife. He asked me if I had a Bible. "I have a brand new one, the very first Bible that I've ever owned in my entire life." That was my answer to him. He asked me to promise to him that I would read the Book of Jonah that very evening. I promised Steve that I would do it, out of curiosity. The following day, he asked me if I had read it. And I asked Steve, "Are you saying to me that I would be swallowed by the whale if I would say "No" to Him? He said, "Something like that will happen to you if you say "No" to the Lord." I could sense the seriousness in his voice. That evening, I requested Luz, Leo, my cousin Mely, my sister-in-law Carmen, and my parents along with Chita, of course, to pray together to ask for direction from the Lord regarding Steve's proposal. During the prayer, words of prophecy came. "My son, Rober, I want you to go in my Name and serve me and the group. Do not be afraid because I am with you. I love that group and I will never leave that group. I am empowering you to serve me by serving my people. Go in my Name, my son. My name is Jesus. My people are waiting for you." The following day, I called Deacon Bill Brennan and told him what had transpired in the past few days. I told him that I had received an invitation to lead the group at St. Luke's and that I felt I wasn't ready to do it yet. I gave him many more reasons and excuses why I should not do it. I also informed him about what I had received in prophecy the previous night when we prayed together with my relatives. I gave him so many reasons of my inadequacy and incompetency in leading a group, period. I was hoping for him to say that I should not do it. In that way, I would not feel bad if I would say "No," and I would be "off the hook," so to speak. He said, "Bob, I think you should go. I discern that the Lord wants you to go to St. Luke's."

The prayer group meets on Saturdays at 2:00 P.M. in the Social Hall. The first prayer meeting that I led was on the second Saturday in March 1985, almost four months to the day after which we had experienced the Baptism in the Holy Spirit. There were only six of us. The following week, only three of us attended. In the next three months, only three, four, or five attended most of the time. I started to feel discouraged and I almost gave up. Besides, we didn't have any music ministry in the group. Not long after that, only two of us were present, looking at each other. The other person was Gene Guiao. He told me that he was a protestant minister. I asked him why he came, and he told me that he didn't know why. He said that he had strong promptings from the Lord to park his car as he was driving by. "The Lord asked me to come inside the building," Pastor Gene told me, after he introduced himself. I told him about the prayer meeting, which was supposed to start at 2:00 P.M., and that nobody had showed up yet except him and me. I suggested that we should start to pray and sing to the Lord while waiting for the others to come.

He told me, "Didn't Jesus say, "When two or three are gathered in my Name, there I am in their midst? We have the minimum number here!" We started to sing praises to the Lord and then, a few minutes later, we started to dance also. The two of us danced all over the hall for over an hour. I went one way and he went the opposite way. The Holy Spirit must have gotten a hold of the two of us because it felt like we could not stop singing and dancing while praising the Lord! Pastor Gene commented afterwards that the Holy Spirit allowed us to have a glimpse of what King David of the Old Testament might have felt while he was singing and dancing before the Lord. "Can you imagine, Bob, that the Lord has chosen the two of us to experience this wonderful thing today, in this place? Isn't this a big blessing for us?" he quipped. I heartily agreed with him. "I believe this is a divine appointment," I retorted back to him. Maybe this would not have happened had there been another person with us today. That's probably why He made sure that there are only two of us here today," I surmised. "I'm sure there were hosts of angels dancing with us. In Psalm 22, we read that God dwells in the praises of His people. Where God is, angels are also there!" I told him further.

For me, that was one of the best prayer meetings I'd ever attended to this day, because we "got lost in the Lord's presence."

In 1986, the members of the prayer group asked the Lord to give our prayer group a name. After invoking the Holy Spirit for guidance, we drew lots to pick out the name that the Lord wanted us to have. The name Children of God Prayer Community was picked from among the various names that were submitted by the members.

People lining up to give their testimony of healing during the Healing Rally in Smyrna Beach, FL. Robert is in the foreground.

CHAPTER SIX

The Operations of the Gifts:

Word of Knowledge, Healing, Miracles, and Prophecy

I n 1 Corinthians 12:4-11, St. Paul asserts,

There are different kinds of spiritual gifts but the same Spirit; there are different forms of service but the same Lord; there are different workings but the same God who produces all of them in everyone. To each individual the manifestation of the Spirit is given for some benefit. To one is given through the Spirit the expression of wisdom; to another the expression of knowledge according to the same Spirit; to another faith by the same Spirit; to another gifts of healing by the one Spirit; to another mighty deeds; to another prophecy; to another discernment of spirits; to another varieties of tongues; to another interpretation of tongues. But one and the same Spirit produces all of these, distributing them individually to each person as he wishes.

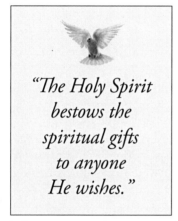

"The Holy Spirit bestows the spiritual gifts to anyone He wishes."

The Holy Spirit bestows the spiritual gifts to anyone He wishes. The main purpose for the operation of these gifts is to build up or edify the body of Christ. The Holy Spirit gives these gifts freely and generously to individuals for service or ministry. Charism is taken from Greek word, "Charismata," which means favor freely given to whomever the Lord chooses. It is not something that the recipient has earned or deserved. Jesus says in Luke 11:13,

> If you then who are wicked, know how to give good gifts to your children, how much more will the Father in heaven give the Holy Spirit to those who ask him?

One Saturday afternoon towards the end of the prayer meeting, I heard a voice in my heart, saying, "My son, I'm healing someone here who could not urinate. Call out and lay hands on that person." I looked around the circle, and there were seven of us, and I was the only male. I said to the Lord in my heart, *Lord, you know quite well that these are all women. I'm embarrassed to say it to them.* Then He said, "I want you to obey me, my son." I was still very hesitant to announce those words. I was debating within myself whether to say it to them. *Suppose no one would come forward, I would look foolish and dumb. Suppose someone would get offended,* I thought to myself. I was also very hesitant to put someone on the spot. I asked the group to sing one more song and then another song. I felt that my heart was beating faster than normal, but finally I could no longer contain those words that I received in my heart. With much hesitation I announced, "The Lord is healing somebody here who could not urinate. Please come in the middle of the circle and we will lay hands on you for complete healing." I really hesitated to say the word "urinate." Helen came forward, saying that she had a urinary tract infection and that she had difficulty urinating because of the pain. Immediately, my anxiety was relieved after Helen came forward. I got so excited that I was praising the Lord for giving me this word of knowledge. Minutes after we had prayed over Helen, she excused herself to go to the restroom. She came out of the restroom with a big smile on her face and told us that she "did it normally without any pain." Helen was completely healed of that infection that very day. Since that day, I have been using the gift of knowledge along with the word of wisdom, prophecy, tongues, healings, miracles, discernment of spirits, speaking in tongues, interpretation of tongues, and other spiritual gifts whenever there is a need for them or when the situations I'm in calls for me to open myself up, to be a receptacle, so to speak, to the operations of these gifts.

One evening I was in St. Nicholas of Tolentine Church in Queens, New York, to conduct a Healing Rally. The church was fully packed. As I was giving a teaching on "Jesus, the Master Healer," I saw a vision with my eyes open of a man holding a shot gun to a woman and two young girls who were probably in their early twenties. I asked the Lord in my heart what this vision was all about. I received an impression that this man had threatened to kill his wife and two daughters. "He felt shame and guilt of what he did to them and he could not forgive himself. "I want you to tell him that I have forgiven him, and that he needs to forgive himself so that he can receive my peace," were the words that I received from the Lord in my heart. Furthermore, I received an impression that this man did not do the evil that he intended to do to his family by the grace of God. I announced this vision to the congregation and I asked this man to come to the aisle of the church so that we could pray with him for emotional healing. No one stood up. I announced it again but still there was no response. I then said, "I know where you are and please don't let me get you." Again, nobody made a move. So, I decided to walk down the aisle towards the entrance of the church, singing "Walking with Jesus, walking everyday, walking all the way." The church was so silent that you could have heard a pin drop. I had friends who were seated close to the front pews and I could see a "horrified look" on their faces. I stopped next to the second pew from the church's entrance. Then I

"The Holy Spirit will never make a mistake."

pointed to the man seated in the middle of the pew. "Brother, it's you, right?" He stood up and he said, "Yes it was me." So I proceeded to tell him of the prophecy or message from the Lord. "Everything you said is true," he told me with tears streaming down his cheeks. I asked the congregation to extend their hands and to pray for emotional and psychological healing for him.

After the Healing Rally was over, my friends came up to me and told me that they were somewhat terrified when I started walking from the foot of the altar towards the entrance of the church. "What you did really required a lot of guts on your part. Suppose you made a mistake; that would have been very embarrassing," they told me. "The Holy Spirit will never make a mistake. I saw a flickering light on top of his head, which indicated to me that was him," I assured them. Thereafter, the Lord gave me names of people, through the gift of the word of knowledge, and I had to call these names out and requested them to stand.

> *"Without a doubt, the gifts of the Holy Spirit are more powerful and more potent than all the weapons combined in this world,..."*

When these people were on their feet, I believe between fifteen to twenty altogether, the Lord gave me a specific message or messages or prophecy for each one of them. Right then and there, they confirmed their respective message or messages. I just repeated what I heard from my "inner being" what the Lord wanted me to say to each one of them. I don't know any one of them, and it was the first time for me to meet them.

In Isaiah 43:1, the Lord God says,

> But now, thus says the LORD, who created you, Jacob, and formed you, Israel: Do not fear, for I have redeemed you; I have called you by name: you are mine.

Yes, indeed the Lord knows us by name and He knows everything about us, even the number of hairs on our body. (cf. Matthew 10:30)

I really felt a very powerful presence of the Lord that evening. As a footnote, I would like to report that about a year later, I saw this man, the one who had threatened his family with a shotgun, again during the Alliance of Filipino Catholic Charismatic Prayer Communities' Regional Convention in East Brunswick, New Jersey. He told me, "Brother Bob, you know, now I am at peace with myself and my relationship with my family could not be better. I am now a changed person and I started to go to church almost daily and read the Bible every day," he said with a smile on his face. Indeed, these spiritual gifts are manifestations of God's love, His presence, and His power. If used with proper discernment and with the anointing of the Holy Spirit, these gifts can change people's lives for the glory of God. Without a doubt, the gifts of the Holy Spirit are more powerful and more potent than all the weapons combined in this world, because they are divine in nature. There is no power in this world that is more powerful than God's power, because God's power is limitless. God's power can build up or destroy any power in this world that doesn't belong to Him. There is no power in this world that could come close to God's power. I've learned through experience that to use the gifts of the Holy Spirit, I have to totally surrender to Him and trust in His power that He wants to manifest through me. We have to obey His promptings, leadings, and nudgings whether it is convenient or inconvenient. It is only by totally surrendering to Him that we can truly be alive in the Lord. Someone said that, "In order to experience the miraculous, we have to be willing to do the ridiculous." I could never forget these words of wisdom. It's not really who we are, but who He is. It is not about us, but it's about the King of Kings and the Lord of Lords, the Alpha and Omega, the Beginning and the End, and the Savior of the world, Jesus Christ our Lord.

The anointing of the Holy Spirit that I had witnessed and experienced in St. Nicholas Tolentine Church has been repeated many times over in many places throughout the world where I have had the privilege and honor to conduct and to speak at Healing Rallies and crusades, workshops, seminars, parish missions, retreats, Days of Renewal, conferences, and conventions. Many times, the anointing is even more powerful and more profound because God is sovereign and His power is unfathomable.

Sometime in 1987, a lady named Lourdes came to the prayer meeting at St. Luke's Parish with her husband, brothers and sisters, and her children. She said she had cancer of the breast, and that it had spread to the lungs. The doctors gave her only six months to live. She was undergoing chemotherapy. So we prayed over her at every prayer meeting for the next three months for the Lord to heal her completely and for the chemotherapy treatment to be effective in treating her without bad after effects of the treatment. One day, she came with the praise reports that her doctors had declared her cancer-free. The news of her healing had spread like wildfire. As a result, many more people started to come to the prayer meeting. Incidentally, Lourdes is cancer-free to this very day. Miracles and healings started to happen even more. Fr. Sebastian Drake and Fr. Tom Alkire, a Carmelite priest from St. Gertrude Parish in Stockton, also started coming weekly to the prayer meeting. As a result, many more people started coming as well to the prayer meeting at St. Luke's Parish in Stockton.

One day, I sensed that a coworker of mine, my fellow auditor-appraiser named Greg, who is always a "gregarious" kind of guy (please pardon the pun) was very quiet. I knew right away that there was something wrong with him because it was very obvious that he was not his usual self. During our coffee break, I approached him and asked him if there was something wrong. He told me that the day before, his mother had suffered a stroke while she was in the airport in London waiting for her flight back to the United States. He said that she was in the hospital. "Can we pray for her, you and I, right now?", I asked him while extending my hands to him at the same time. With some hesitation, he grabbed my hands and then we prayed. As we were praying for his mom, I told him that the Lord gave me a vision of this lady. Then I described the vision about how this lady looked; the color and the style of her hair, the color of dress she was wearing, and the kind of purse she was using. Greg told me that I was describing his mom to him. "I'm amazed that you saw my mom in a vision, and you described her to me with great accuracy, even though you haven't met her," Greg told me. "It's God, Greg, and this is what He said to you as we were praying, "My son, worry not because I am healing your mother. Continue to pray for her in my Name. My Name is Jesus. I love you my son." A few days later, Greg told me with excitement in his voice that his mom was released from the hospital and that she was fine. "As a matter of fact, she is now re-scheduling her flight back to California," Greg happily reported to me. Because of this experience, I started to pray with people with more enthusiasm and more expectant faith than ever before. I could not thank the Lord enough for letting the gifts of the word of knowledge, word of wisdom, healing, miracles, prophecy, and other spiritual gifts be very active in my life in spite of myself.

I have developed a habit over the years that wherever I am, I always pray in tongues, "under my breath," most of the time. I believe this is one of the graces that the Holy Spirit has bestowed upon me. I also found it to be one of the most effective ways for me to refocus my heart and mind on the Lord when I get distracted. One day, my wife asked me to do grocery shopping. As I grabbed the grocery cart, I started to pray in tongues under my breath. Then the Lord spoke into my heart as I was walking towards the grocery's produce section. He said, "My son, Rober, do you see that lady about two o'clock from where you are?" "Yes, Lord, I see her." "Go and talk to her in my Name," was His terse instruction. "About what Lord?" "I will give you the words to say to her." The lady was looking over a pile of potatoes. So I stood next to her, looking over a pile of tomatoes.

"Oh, the prices of potatoes and tomatoes seem to be going higher and higher almost every week, huh?" I said to her after a few minutes just to start a conversation with her. "I think you're right," she said approvingly. After talking with her about the prices of other commodities, I introduced myself to her, and she also gave me her name. I asked her, "Do you mind if I ask you a personal question?" "No, what kind of question do you have in mind?"

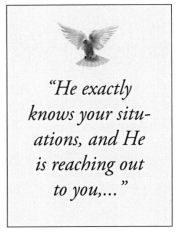

"He exactly knows your situations, and He is reaching out to you,..."

she asked me. "Is there anything that happened in your life recently for which you could use some prayers?" I asked her without hesitation.

Suddenly, she looked at me straight in the eyes and tears started flowing down her cheeks. "You know, I lost my husband three months ago, and it is very painful. I'm distraught and depressed. I seem to be lost. I feel so alone without him. We were very close to each other. I don't know what to do." "I'm very sorry to hear that. But if you want, I can pray with you, and we can ask the Lord to give you comfort and peace, but of course, it is all up to you," was my immediate response to her.

"Well, sure, if it's okay with you." So we held hands over the pile of potatoes and tomatoes and we started praying. Then the Lord spoke into my heart again as we were praying, "Tell her that my love for her doesn't end. Tell her to rejoice and to be joyful because her husband is in my hands. I also have plans for her. Let her know that I want her to trust in my love for her. From now on, I am her father, her mother, her sister, her husband, her brother, her shield, her protector, her life." Then I received a vision of this man wearing a plaid shirt and a ten-gallon hat and pair of cowboy boots. I relayed the messages and this vision to her. "You are describing my husband to me. This is incredible," she said with a big smile on her face. "My God, thank you for telling me those words of comfort. I really needed to hear those words bad. Wow, this is incredible, it's mind boggling." "Just keep on praising and thanking the Lord for His goodness and love for you. The Lord exactly knows your situations, and He is reaching out to you. You know, He's crazy about you, He is crazy about all of His children," I assured her.

As a result, this lady's personal demeanor had changed dramatically, from being "gloomy" to being "spritely" looking. She also could not stop thanking me. In addition, this experience had tremendously increased my faith in the saving, loving, and healing power of the Lord.

I believe it's God's will that the gifts of the Holy Spirit should be used freely wherever and whenever they are needed to build up His Kingdom and to draw His people unto Himself.

CHAPTER SEVEN

Official Launching of the Healing Ministry by the Lord

I n the spring of 1989, I was invited to conduct a Healing service outside of California for the first time during the National Convention of the Filipino-American Prayer Communities in Norfolk, Virginia. The Lord healed many who came, including a lady who walked from her wheelchair and deaf people who could hear again, not to mention various other healings such as healings of upper and lower backs, migraine headaches, healings of "frozen shoulders," and other healings too numerous to mention. Moreover, I noticed the gift of prophecy really started to operate through me in a very powerful way, in spite of my limitations, while I prayed for the sick. I just repeated the words that I received in my heart to the person that I was ministering to. For instance, while I was praying for one particular lady, I received these words from the Lord telling her, "My daughter know that I love you. I want you to forgive your husband and continue to love and honor him. Give him to me because I know what to do with him. Trust in me, my daughter, because my love for you and your husband will never fade away." After we prayed, she told me that their marriage was on the "rocks." She said she had difficulty forgiving her husband of what he did to her. As a result, I prayed for the Holy Spirit to give her the grace to forgive her husband fully, in light of the words of prophecy that I had received for her. For sure, the gifts of the Holy Spirit had not only built up my faith in the love and power of the Lord, but they had also built up the faith of many with whom I had come in contact. I believe that the Lord used this event to launch officially the healing ministry that He had promised to grant me on December 8, 1984.

During that convention, I received at least three invitations from the different prayer groups in different parts of the United States to come to their respective places to conduct teachings and healing services. My faith that the Lord can and will use me to heal in His name in spite of myself has "skyrocketed" because of this experience. In 1991, I was invited for the first time to speak at the International Catholic Charismatic Conference in Manila, Philippines, exactly seven years after I received the Baptism in the Holy Spirit.

When this invitation came, my wife Chita was praying about this while she was attending Mass at St. Luke's

Parish one day. Chita said that she had a vision as clear as day, or mental picture, of the Lord Jesus in front of her, holding my briefcase. She said this took place while she was praying before the Blessed Sacrament after the Holy Sacrifice of the Mass. "Would you give me permission to let your husband travel with me?" the Lord asked her. "Yes, Lord, whatever is your will for us," Chita said was her response to the Lord Jesus. According to her, the Lord thanked

"People walked from their wheelchairs, people threw away their canes and walkers and ran around inside the auditoriums praising and thanking God."

her for giving Him the permission. "Can you imagine, the Lord of Lords, the King of Kings, the Creator of the universe, the everlasting God asking my permission and then thanking me for giving Him the permission to let you travel with Him?" my wife excitedly shared with me her experience. "The Lord is not only very humble but He is very gentle and loving and He really respects our free will," I retorted back to her. She said it was indeed a very humbling and very uplifting experience. It was the first time for me to minister outside of the United States. I did not only minister in the city of Manila but also in Quezon City, Makati City, Cebu City, the place where I was born and raised, Iloilo City, and Davao City. It was the first time for me to minister to thousands of people in Jesus' Name. It was the first time for me to witness in great number. People walked from their wheelchairs, people threw away their canes and walkers and ran around inside the auditoriums praising and thanking God. The blind saw, the deaf mute became able to hear and speak, tumors and abnormal growths disappeared instantly.

During one of the Healing Crusades in Quezon City, I was praying over a lady who had a goiter tumor as big as a lemon fruit protruding from her neck. She rested in the Spirit for about five minutes after I prayed over her. When she got up from the floor, she was grasping her neck, saying, "What happened to my goiter?" "What happened to my goiter?" When she took her hands off her neck, everyone around her was amazed because the lemon-sized goiter tumor had disappeared, and her neck looked normal as normal could be, glory be to God! It looked like she was still not convinced of its disappearance because she was touching and feeling the back of her head down to the back of her neck.

"Ma'am, do not look for that goiter tumor anymore. It's already gone. The Lord already took care of it, in His goodness and mercy for you," I assured her. The atmosphere inside that auditorium was electric and saturated with God's presence and power!

CHAPTER EIGHT

Fulfillment of the Prophecy

In September 1989, the Core group of the Children of God Prayer Community had discerned that the Lord wanted the prayer group to conduct a Mass and Miracle Service monthly. They decided also to start publishing a newsletter and named it, *The Shepherd's Voice.*

The prayer group then began to conduct a monthly Mass and Miracle Service in November 1989. This is still going on strong to this very day. Signs and wonders, miracles and healings have been taking place during the prayer meetings and during the Mass and Miracle Service. Many have come from far and wide, even from other states, to experience the healing touch of the Lord. The blind saw, the lame walked, the deaf heard, and cysts and tumors disappeared. People who

"To date, I've been to fifty countries ministering in Jesus' Name."

had been in bondage to various addictions, or had suffered chronic depressions and other emotional maladies, and those who had been oppressed by demonic spirits have been set free. But most of all, many people's lives have been changed by the Lord Jesus after they attended the prayer meetings, miracle services, and other events such as the Life in the Spirit Seminars, Growth In the Spirit Seminars, Days of Renewal, and other evangelistic activities. Many have come to know Jesus as the Healer of the body, mind, soul, and spirit. Many have accepted Him as their Lord and Savior. In Matthew 9:35, God's Word says,

> Jesus went around to all the towns and villages, teaching in their synagogues, proclaiming the gospel of the kingdom, and curing every disease and illness.

One Saturday afternoon during a Mass and Miracle Service in the gym at St. Luke's Parish, a tall, slender gentleman came forward to give his testimony. He said that he was a truck driver from Las Vegas, Nevada, and that six months earlier he had stopped in a restaurant in Stockton for lunch on the way from Reno, Nevada, to Los Angeles, California. While in the restaurant, he said he had tried to get the *San Francisco Chronicle* from the newspaper dispenser. However, the dispenser was jammed, so instead he decided to get *The Record*. He read in *The Record* that a Mass and Miracle Service was to be held at 2:00 P.M. that day. He said, "For some reason, I had a very strong prompting to attend the Mass and Miracle Service at St. Luke's." He said he went up for prayers with some reluctance. "As Bob Canton and other members of the healing team laid hands on me, I fell down backwards on the floor and I had stayed down there for at least ten to fifteen minutes," he explained. He said he had felt like his body was on fire as he was lying down on the floor. Then he said I told him, "This is what the Lord is saying to you, 'My son, trust in me and have faith in me. I'm setting you free from your bondages.'" "No one knew that I had been stoned with heroin for eighteen long years," he confessed with tears in his eyes. "That very day, I stopped taking heroin, cold turkey. I have not taken any heroin since then, and the greatest miracle was that I had no withdrawal symptoms whatsoever! It must be Jesus who did it for me," he emphatically said. "My life has never been the same since then. Yes, I'm putting back my life in order only by the grace of God!"

Yes, the Lord had set him free from long years of drug addiction and, of course, from darkness, alleluia! John 8:36 says, "If the Son of God sets you free, you are free indeed!"

The Lord Jesus has opened doors for me to minister in five continents of the world. I have been witnessing signs and wonders, healings and miracles in ways that I had never thought possible before. It has been a glorious experience to be a witness, to be at the "ringside seat," so to speak, and watch the works of the Lord through the power of the Holy Spirit. The prophecies that I had received back on December 8, 1984, have been fulfilled! However, the total fulfillment of the prophecy is still unfolding. I believe that the Lord is still pouring out more graces and blessings on this ministry, in spite of myself. With the Lord, there is always something more! I could hardly wait to witness and experience more healings, more miracles, and more conversions of hearts and minds in the Name of Jesus and by the power of the Holy Spirit, because our Heavenly Father is a miracle-working God. I also believe that the Lord Jesus can and will use this book, in spite of myself, to heal and to touch anyone who prays with expectant faith any prayer contained in this book. Jesus says in Luke 17:6,

> If you have faith the size of a mustard seed, you would say to this mulberry tree, 'Be uprooted and planted in the sea,' and it would obey you.

I was employed by San Joaquin County as Senior Auditor-Appraiser. In 2006, I received strong promptings from the Lord to take an early retirement from my job and work full time for Him. I kept on bargaining with the Lord, telling Him that I was not ready yet to retire. Besides, I was still too young to retire. I thank the Lord that He was very patient with me. He is always patient with all of His children. Finally in 2008, when my children had all graduated from college, the Lord reminded me again to work full time for Him. In April 2008, I heeded the Lord's request and decided to take an early retirement from my job with the backing of my wife. Soon afterwards, many invitations not only from North America but also from the different countries throughout the world came pouring in.

Speaking before the Brazilian National Catholic Charismatic Conference in Foz Iguazzo. Next to Robert is Katia Roldi, the Portuguese translator.

Part of the 8,000 attendees of the Brazilian National Catholic Charismatic Conference in Foz Iguazzo.

CHAPTER NINE

Overview of the Charism of Healing and Prayer for Healing

J esus' first instructions to His disciples had been, As you go, make this proclamation: The kingdom of heaven is at hand. Cure the sick, raise the dead, cleanse lepers, drive out demons." (Matthew 10:7-8)

In John 14:12, Jesus says,

Amen, amen, I say to you, whoever believes in me will do the works that I do, and will do greater ones than these, because I am going to the Father.

Jesus also states,

But you will receive power when the Holy Spirit comes upon you, and you will be my witnesses in Jerusalem, throughout Judea and Samaria, and to the ends of the earth. (Acts 1:8)

The Lord is always true to His promises. In the Catholic Charismatic Renewal, the Lord has raised up many men and women, members of the clergy, and religious and lay people who have very active ministries of healing. Healing is one of the spiritual gifts mentioned in the book of 1 Corinthians 12, which serve and edify the Church.

Purposes of the Healing Ministry

In my ministry of preaching, teaching, and healing, I perceive the following purposes for the Healing Ministry:

1. ***To give evidence that the Gospel is the Word of God and that Jesus is alive.*** In the scriptures we read that Jesus healed all kinds of sicknesses, all types of disease, and all sick people who came to Him for healing. He is the Healer par excellence. Matthew 4:23-25 reads, "He went around all of Galilee, teaching in their synagogues, proclaiming the Gospel of the kingdom, and curing every disease and illness among the people. His fame

spread to all of Syria, and they brought to him all who were sick with various diseases and racked with pain, those who were possessed, lunatics, and paralytics, and he cured them. And great crowds from Galilee, the Decapolis, Jerusalem, and Judea, and from beyond the Jordan followed him.

2. *To demonstrate that God's Kingdom is at hand.* God's Kingdom is here and now. Every time divine healing takes place and the oppressed are set free, then the Kingdom of God is present. "But if it is by the finger of God that I drive out demons, then the kingdom of God has come upon you." (Luke 11:20)

3. *To bring glory and honor to God.* In Luke 17:12-19, we read" As he was entering a village, ten lepers met Him. They stood at a distance from him and raised their voice, saying, "Jesus, Master! Have pity on us!"And when he saw them, he said, "Go show yourselves to the priests." As they were going they were cleansed. And one of them, realizing he had been healed, returned, glorifying God in a loud voice; and he fell at the feet of Jesus and

thanked him. He was a Samaritan. Jesus said in reply, "Ten were cleansed, were they not? Where are the other nine? Has none but this foreigner returned to give thanks to God?" Then he said to him, "Stand up and go; your faith has saved you." Matthew 15:30-31 reads, "Great crowds came to him, having with them the lame, the blind, the deformed, the mute, and many others. They placed them at his feet, and he cured them. The crowds were amazed when they saw the mute speaking, the deformed made whole, the lame walking, and the blind able to see, and they glorified the God of Israel."

4. ***To draw people to Jesus and bring them to salvation.*** People came to know Jesus as their Lord and their Savior because they experienced His power and His healing touch. In Matthew 9:9-12, we read, "As Jesus passed on from there, he saw a man named Matthew sitting at the customs post. He said to him, "Follow me." And he got up and followed him. While he was at table in his house, many tax collectors and sinners came and sat with Jesus and his disciples. The Pharisees saw this and said

to his disciples, "Why does your teacher eat with tax collectors and sinners?" He heard this and said, "Those who are well do not need a physician, but the sick do.

5. ***To show God's love, compassion, and mercy, and to relieve human suffering.*** In the ministry of Jesus, we see it is His nature to heal and He cannot stand seeing people suffer. "A leper came to him and kneeling down begged him and said, "If you wish, you can make me clean. Moved with pity, he stretched out his hand, touched him, and said to him, "I do will it. Be made clean." (Mark 1:40-41)

6. ***As fulfillment of God's promises.*** In Matthew 8:16-17, the Word of God says, "When it was evening, they brought him many who were possessed by demons, and he drove out the spirits by a word and cured all the sick, to fulfill what had been said by Isaiah the prophet: "He took away our infirmities and bore our diseases."

7. ***To demonstrate once again Jesus' victory on the Cross over the evil one.*** Acts 10:37-38, says, "How God anointed Jesus of Nazareth with the Holy Spirit

and power. He went about doing good and healing all those oppressed by the devil, for God was with him." The Word of God also says in 1 John 3:8, "Whoever sins belongs to the devil, because the devil has sinned from the beginning. Indeed, the Son of God was revealed to destroy the works of the devil."

Teaching of the Roman Catholic Church Regarding Healing

The Catechism of the Catholic Church asserts that "Christ's compassion toward the sick and his many healings of every kind of infirmity are a resplendent sign that "God has visited His people" and that the Kingdom of God is close at hand. Jesus has the power not only to heal, but also to forgive sins; he has come to heal the whole man, soul and body; he is the physician the sick have need of" (1504).

In the book, *Instruction On Prayers For Healing*, published by the Congregation for the Doctrine of the Faith, we read, "Christ's meeting with the sick is one of the most human aspects we find in the Gospels. This meeting is for the total, global salvation of the person, and not only to bring bodily health alone, overcome physical sickness and hence avoid "becoming bogged down in the impossible aim of finally defeating death." The meeting between Christ and the sick, is, both in the Gospels and still today, to heal the person in his or her totality, and hence with a dimension of eternity."

Pope Benedict XV1, in his book, *Jesus of Nazareth*, writes that "Healing is an essential dimension of the apostolic mission and of Christian faith in general."

It can even be said that Christianity is a "therapeutic religion, a religion of healing. When understood at a sufficiently deep level, this expresses the entire content of redemption." Salvation in Christ is ultimately a healing of humanity's deepest wound: the wound of our sin and consequent alienation from God. Conversely, the fullness of healing is forgiveness of sin and the restoration of communion with God."

According to the *Guidelines of Prayer For Healing*, a booklet published by the Doctrinal Commission of the International Catholic Charismatic Renewal Services (ICCRS), with the approval of the Congregation of the Doctrine of the Faith, there are four basic categories of healing, namely physical healing: the healing from physical sickness and disability; psychological healing: the healing of wounds to the human psyche, including emotional wounds; spiritual healing: this means, above all, the "healing from sin" that restores a person to a relationship with God; and exorcism and deliverance.

Ministering during the Healing Crusade in Sibu, Sarawak, Malaysia. James Blubaugh is the man behind the sick being ministered to.

Part of the attendees during the Healing Crusade in Sacred Heart Cathedral, Sibu, Sarawak, Malaysia.

CHAPTER TEN

How to Pray for Healing and Achieve Results

In exercising the ministry of preaching, teaching, and healing in many countries throughout the world, I can attest that healing the sick in the Name of Jesus is one of the most effective tools for evangelization. I have witnessed people who came to know the loving and the saving power of the Lord Jesus Christ through the ministry of healing.

> These signs will accompany those who believe: in my Name they will drive out demons, they will speak new languages, they will pick up serpents, and if they drink any deadly thing, it will not harm them. They will lay hands on the sick, and they will recover." (Mark 16:17-18)

In the light of what Jesus said, any baptized believer can pray for the sick. While it is true and generally accepted that there are particular charisms of healings given only to some, this should not preclude any baptized Christian from praying for the sick.

The following are some ways to pray for healing, especially physical healing, and achieve results. This list is by no means exhaustive nor exclusive.

How to Pray for Healing

1. *Have a constant, personal, intimate, day-by-day, and moment-by-moment relationship and fellowship with the Lord.* Without this kind of relationship with the Lord, one's life is devoid of real power. In John 15:5; 7, Jesus asserts, "I am the vine, you are the branches. Whoever remains in me, and I in him, will bear much fruit, because without me you can do nothing." "If you remain in me, and my words remain in you, ask for whatever you will, and it will be given unto you."

2. *Avail yourself with the Sacraments of the Church, especially the Sacraments of Reconciliation and the Eucharist.* The healing minister may encourage the sick to do the same. These are the most

powerful sources of healing, including the Sacrament of the Anointing of the Sick. The Catechism of the Catholic Church (1509) states, "The Church believes in the life-giving presence of Christ, the Physician of souls and bodies. This presence is particularly active through the Sacraments, and in an altogether special way through the Eucharist, the bread that gives eternal life and that St. Paul suggests is connected with bodily health."

3. *Always say a "protective" prayer before the healing session to prevent any contamination or transference of spirits of affliction and infirmity into anyone.* A prayer of command invoking the Name and the blood of Jesus for protection and to bind any spirit of harassment and retaliation is recommended.

4. *Invoke Mary, the Mother of God, and the holy angels for their intercession and protection.* The Catechisms of the Catholic Church, 968, states, "Mary's role in relation to the Church and to all humanity goes still further. "In a wholly singular way she cooperated by her obedience, faith, hope, and burning charity

in the Savior's work of restoring supernatural life to souls. For this reason, she
is a mother to us in the order of grace."

5. *Have an expectant faith.* (Luke 17:6)
   Have faith that the Lord can work in and
   through you for His glory.

6. *Ask questions and listen attentively to
   the person you are ministering to before
   you start praying.* Information such as
   the kind of sickness the person is suffering from, the doctor's diagnosis, and
   the person's faith in the healing power of
   Jesus may guide you on how to proceed
   in praying for that person.

7. *Lay hands on the sick.* Jesus laid hands
   on the sick and healed them. However,
   proper discretion should be used on the
   laying on of hands. "He took the blind
   man by the hand and led him outside
   the village. Putting spittle on his eyes
   he laid his hands on him and asked,
   "Do you see anything?" Looking up he
   replied, "I see people looking like trees
   and walking. Then he laid hands on his
   eyes a second time and he saw clearly;
   his sight was restored and he could see

everything distinctly." (Mark 8:23-25 When I lay hands on the sick, I'm allowing the power of the Lord to flow through my hands into the sick person. My hands cannot heal. Only the Lord's hands can heal. My hands are just a point of contact, a conduit, so to speak, of the healing power from the Lord to the sick person.

8. *Be specific in your prayers; the more specific the prayers, the better.* In Matthew 7:7-11, Jesus says, "Ask and it will be given to you; seek and you will find; knock and the door will be opened to you. For everyone who asks, receives; and the one who seeks, finds; and to the one who knocks, the door will be opened. Which one of you would hand his son a stone when he asks for a loaf of bread, or a snake when he asks for a fish? If you then, who are wicked, know how to give good gifts to your children, how much more will your heavenly Father give good things to those who ask him. "One day, while Jesus was walking on the streets of Jericho, two blind men who were sitting by the roadside, shouted at Jesus, saying, "Lord, Son of David, have mercy on us." Jesus

stopped upon hearing them, and asked them, "What do you want me to do for you?" They said to Jesus, "Lord, we want to see!" (Matthew 20:30-33). Jesus knew that they were blind, but He still asked them specifically, what they had wanted Him to do for them.

9. *Use the Name of Jesus.* There is power in the Name of Jesus. "If you ask anything of me in my Name, I will do it." (John 14:14) "Therefore, God has highly exalted him and has given him the name which is above every name, that at the name of Jesus every knee should bow, in heaven and on earth and under the earth, and every tongue confess that Jesus Christ is Lord, to the glory of God the Father." (Philippians 2:9-11) When we speak the name of Jesus with expectant faith and conviction and with great reverence, power and anointing are released by the Holy Spirit.

10. *Be open to the Holy Spirit and His gifts, especially prophecy, word of knowledge, word of wisdom, and discernment of spirits.* These are great tools in conducting the ministry of healing. I have experienced over and over again that anointed

word of knowledge and prophecy by the Holy Spirit often have impacted the lives of many.

11. ***Obey the voice of the Lord.*** Obey the leadings and the promptings of the Holy Spirit. "Obedience is better than sacrifice, submission than the fat of rams. (1 Samuel 15:22) We should strive to have ears to hear the voice of the Lord and obey his promptings and commands. In other words, we should open wide the ears of our heart so that we may be able to listen clearly to his words.

12. ***"Call the things that are not as though they were."*** (Romans 4:17) I personally describe it as a "build-up prayer." An example of such a prayer is to ask the Lord for brand new eyes for the blind or brand new eardrums and auditory nerves for the deaf, and so forth. "For God, nothing is impossible at all." (Luke 1:37)

13. ***Ask Jesus to apply his precious blood and his healing touch into the diseased parts of the person's body.*** "By His stripes, we were healed." (Isaiah 53:5)

14. **"Seal" the healing with the blood and the Name of Jesus and the mantle of the Virgin Mary so that the healing may last.** This could prevent symptoms and the sickness itself from recurring.

15. **Pray a "cleansing prayer" after the healing session.** This prayer is intended to prevent any entity or spirit of infirmity and/or spirit of retaliation to attach itself to anyone involved in the healing prayer. Prayers for refreshment of mind and body and renewed anointing from the Holy Spirit are also desirable at this time.

16. **Give praise to God's goodness and His healing love.** "Through him, let us continually offer God a sacrifice of praise that is the fruit of lips that confess his name." (Hebrews 13:15) The Lord God says that He dwells in the praises of His people (cf. Psalm 22).

God is the creator as well as the Healer of our body, mind, soul, and spirit. In Psalm 139:13-18, God's words say,

> For you created my inmost being; you knit me together in my mother's womb. I praise you because I am fearfully and wonderfully

made; your works are wonderful, I know
that full well. My frame was not hidden
from you when I was made in the secret
place, when I was woven together in the
depths of the earth. Your eyes saw my
unformed body; all the days ordained for
me were written in your book before one of
them came to be. How precious to me are
your thoughts, God! How vast is the sum
of them! Were I to count them, they would
outnumber the grains of sand when I awake,
I am still with you.

I believe that the Lord can use anyone and anything
to heal. Of course, He uses doctors and medicines also
to heal His people. Doctors and medicines are certainly
God's gifts to us. In the book of Sirach 38:1-9, we read,

Hold the physician in honor, for he is
essential to you, and God it was who
established his profession.

From God the doctor has his wisdom, and
the king provides for his sustenance.

His knowledge makes the doctor
distinguished, and gives him access to
those in authority. God makes the earth
yield healing herbs which the prudent
man should not neglect; Was not the water

sweetened by a twig that men might learn his power?

He endows men with the knowledge to glory in his mighty works,

Through which the doctor eases pain and the druggist prepares his medicines;

Thus God's creative work continues without cease in its efficacy on the surface of the earth. My son, when you are ill, delay not, but pray to God, who will heal you.

When we are sick, of course we pray to God for healing and seek the help of a physician, most especially when the sickness is of a serious nature. It will also help a great deal if we ask the Holy Spirit to give the doctor the wisdom to come up with the accurate diagnosis and to guide and direct him on how to treat us and to prescribe for us proper and effective medications for our illness. In this vein, I suggest that we should pray over the medication, thanking the Lord for it and asking him to take away any after-effects or bad effects that may cause harm to our body, before taking it.

During Healing Crusades and Healing Rallies that I have had the privilege to conduct, I always made it a point to remind people that they should not stop taking medications prescribed by their doctors because they feel they are already "healed." We should not practice medicine without a license. I suggest that doctors should verify healings as much as possible. I believe that this is a prudent thing to do and this will, for sure, give more glory and honor to the Lord.

Yes, there are healings that are instantaneous in nature. There are also healings that are on an "installment basis." To persevere in prayer and to continually praise and thank the Lord for His goodness and for His love and for His healing touch will reap blessings far beyond our wildest imaginations.

Jesus was the Healer par excellence while He was still walking on this Earth because He was filled and empowered by the Holy Spirit. He was truly God and He was truly man. In His humanity, He had to rely on the leadings and promptings of the Holy Spirit to do what He did. The Father's will is for us to conform to the image and likeness of His Son. Let us, therefore, raise our voices to our Heavenly Father and continually implore Him for the grace to help us become more like His Son Jesus Christ in every way.

During the Catholic Charismatic Conference in Miami, FL

CHAPTER ELEVEN

Possible Roadblocks to Healing

I have mentioned in the previous chapters of this book that I have witnessed so many miracles and healings and restoration and deliverance done in the mighty Name of Jesus and by the power of the Holy Spirit.

However, there were many also who have failed to receive their healings. Why? Let us look at some of the possible roadblocks to the healing that the Lord wants us to receive.

Possible Roadblocks

1. *Unforgiveness, Hatred, Bitterness, and Resentment:* In Mark 11:25-26, Jesus says, "When you stand to pray, forgive anyone against whom you have a grievance, so that your Heavenly Father may in turn forgive you your transgressions." In Matthew 6:14-15, the Lord states, "If you forgive others their transgressions, your Heavenly Father will forgive you. But if you do not forgive others, neither will your Father forgive your transgressions."

   Many struggle on this issue of forgiveness. It is not easy to do. However, it is a matter of the will, a conscious decision to forgive. Unforgiveness, hatred, bitterness, and resentment are not only some of the biggest blockages to healing but they are also blamed by health experts and pinpointed by recent scientific studies as possible causes of some physical, emotional, mental, and psychological sickness.

One late evening, back in 2002, in a hotel in the city of Makati, the Philippines, as I was about to retire for the night after conducting workshops and Healing Rallies the whole day, I heard a knock on my door. It was a friend of mine, named Marico Enriquez, who flew with me from San Francisco, California, to witness the Healing Rallies and Crusades in the Philippines. With him, were two ladies. Marico introduced me to Dr. Santiago and to another lady physician. He said these ladies were long time friends of his family. He was very apologetic for bothering me when I was about to go to sleep and he asked if I would pray for Dr. Santiago who had been diagnosed with cancer of the uterus, which metastasized to the lungs. "Bob, her doctor only gave her six months to live," Marico informed me. "Come inside the room, and it is my great honor to pray for you, Dr. Santiago," I told her. I also asked Marico and the other lady physician to pray with me.

I led the three of them to pray the Healing and Keeping Prayer. Afterwards, I laid hands on Dr. Santiago and prayed in tongues. Then the Lord spoke into my heart. "My son, Rober, tell her to forgive George." I said, "Lord, who is George?" "You will find out when you tell her what I have just told you," the Lord said. "Dr. Santiago, the Lord just spoke into my heart and He asked me to tell you to forgive George. Who is George?" I promptly asked her out of curiosity. Dr. Santiago seemed to get startled and she looked at me straight in the eyes for a few seconds. Then tears started flowing down her cheeks. "George is my brother-in-law. I have not spoken to him for at least ten years. We had had a falling out of relationship as a result of some petty things," she informed me. "Where is he now?" I

"Unforgiveness, bitterness, resentment, and hatred are toxins to our physical as well as our spiritual well-being,..."

inquired of her. "He is around. Sometimes I see him in church. However, he goes one way, and I go the opposite way. We just ignore each other," Dr. Santiago said sadly. "Now, the Lord says that you have to forgive him. What can you say about that?" I kind of challenged her. "For sure, I have to do it. I believe what you said to me is from God. Who am I to go against what the Lord wants me to do. You don't know George, and George doesn't know you. And we just met for the first time. That's why I'm wondering how did you know about George and our situations?" Dr. Santiago inquired, while wiping tears from her eyes. "Dr. Santiago, Jesus spoke into my heart through the power of the Holy Spirit," I answered her. I believe He wants you to be spiritually, physically, emotionally, and mentally healed through the power of His Holy Spirit. The Lord loves you so much, Dr. Santiago, and He knows what's going on in our lives," I assured her. "Unforgiveness, bitterness, resentment, and hatred are toxins to our physical as well as our spiritual well-being, as you probably know," I further stated. Thereafter, I led her to say the "Forgiveness" prayer and then proceeded to pray for her for healing of cancer. "It's a good thing that you are willing to forgive your brother-in-law. Otherwise, had you refused to forgive him, I would not have prayed for you. "Why is that?" she inquired. "We can pray all day and all night, but if a person refuses to forgive, it will not do us any good. It will just be an exercise in futility because Jesus says in Mark 11:25, "When you stand to pray, forgive anyone against whom you have a grievance, so that your heavenly Father may in turn forgive you your transgressions," was my reply to her.

About one and a half years later, I received a call from Southern California. "Is this Bob Canton?" the person on the other line inquired. "Yes, speaking!" "Bob, this is Dr. Santiago from Manila, a friend of Marico." "Do you remember me,?" "I sure do!" "Bob, I called to let you know that I'm totally healed of cancer. I heard that you are going to be in Southern California this weekend to speak and to conduct a Healing Service during the Southern California Catholic Charismatic Convention (SCRC). So I came from the Philippines to surprise you. Then I heard that it already took place a week ago," she informed me.

"Bob, I want to let you know that the day after you prayed with me in the hotel, I went straight to my brother-in-law George's house. I asked forgiveness from him. He also asked forgiveness from me. We have reconciled, Bob. We are now on speaking terms again, and so are the members of my family and his family. Oh, Bob what a feeling! A heavy burden was finally lifted from our families. But the best news Bob is this: my doctors have declared me cancer-free about six months ago. The cancer just disappeared," Dr. Santiago informed me. "Praise God, He is really good, and He is the Master Healer!" I exclaimed with excitement. This experience convinced me even more to preach about the importance of forgiveness as an ingredient to healing and wholeness.

   2. ***Lack of Faith:*** In Hebrews 11:1, St. Paul says, "Faith is the realization of what is hoped for and evidence of things not seen." In Matthew 21:22, Jesus says, "Whatever you ask for in prayer with faith, you will receive."

   Unbelief is a big roadblock to healing. Sometimes, people don't get healed because they don't believe in God's provision and promise of healing. When Jesus went back to His hometown in Nazareth, Scripture says, He was not able to perform mighty deeds there, apart from curing a few sick people by laying hands on them. He was amazed by their lack of faith." St. Paul says, in Hebrews 11:6, "But without faith, it is impossible to please God, for anyone who approaches

God must believe that He exists and that He rewards those who seek Him." If you lack faith or if you want your faith to increase, ask the Holy Spirit, the giver of gifts, to grant you the gift of faith. Faith is one of the gifts of the Holy Spirit as mentioned in 1 Corinthians 12:9.

Sometimes people who lack faith also receive a healing from God. Why? Possible reasons would be the faith of the healing minister and the faith of the people attending the service or the prayer of the intercessory group usher in God's favor.

I remember this man from Jersey City who was healed of a chronic back pain, which he had been suffering with for many years. He said he attended our Healing Rally to please his wife. He said he did not believe that he would be healed or anyone for that matter. He thought that a Healing Rally was a "scam." He said he had not been to church for at least twenty to twenty-five years. He told me when I saw him again a few years later that he became a better Christian and a regular churchgoer after he had received his healing.

3. ***Unrepented Sin or Habitual Sin***: The Catechism of the Catholic Church defines sin as an "offence against reason,

truth, and right conscience; it is a failure in genuine love for God and neighbor caused by a perverse attachment to certain goods." St. Augustine defined sin "as an utterance, a deed or a desire contrary to the eternal law." In Romans 6:23, St. Paul says, "the wages of sin is death." Unrepented and habitual sin is a major block to God healing a person. In James 5:16, God's Word says, "Therefore, confess your sins to one another and pray for one another, that you may be healed. The fervent prayer of a righteous person is very powerful."

Once, Jesus healed a man who had been lame for thirty-eight years, sitting by the pool of Bethesda. "Afterwards, Jesus saw him in the temple area and said to him, "Look you are well; do not sin anymore, so that nothing worse may happen to you." (John 5:14)

Another example was a lame man who was lowered through the roof in Capernaum. Jesus told the lame man, "Child, your sins are forgiven." (Mark 2:5) Sad to say, many in the world today, including Christians, have lost a sense of sin. For instance, sexual sins are very prevalent nowadays, such as pre-marital sex, extra-marital sex, same gender sex, bestiality, prostitution, and pornography.

4. *Taking the Body and Blood of the Lord Unworthily:* In 1 Cor. 11:27-30, "Therefore, whoever eats the bread or drinks the cup of the Lord unworthily will have to answer for the body and blood of the Lord. A person should examine himself, and so eat the bread and drink the cup. For anyone who eats and drinks without discerning the body, eats and drinks judgment on himself. That is why many among you are ill and infirm, and a considerable number are dying."

Receiving the body and blood of Jesus unworthily has some grave consequences. We have to be under grace when receiving communion. On the other hand, if we receive communion in a worthy manner, it is a source of healing and restoration and grace. The Catechism of the Catholic Church states that "the Eucharist is the source and summit of our Christian life." Jesus' body and blood, soul, and divinity are present in the Eucharist. There is no better source of healing than Jesus Himself.

5. ***Failure to Care the Body Properly***: Our body is a temple of the Holy Spirit. If we don't take care of our body properly, chances are we get sick. If we are not getting enough rest and sleep, not getting good nutrition, not drinking enough water, not getting proper exercise, and as a result we get sick, God will not answer our prayer if we persist on not correcting this failure on our part.

6. ***Involvement with Occultism***: Occultism is defined as something that is "Mysterious." In Deuteronomy 18:10-14, the Lord God says, "Let there not be found among you, anyone who immolates his son or daughter in the fire nor a fortune teller, soothsayer, charmer, diviner, or caster of spells, nor one who consults ghosts and spirits or seeks oracles from the dead. Anyone who does such things is an abomination to the Lord, and because of such abominations the Lord, your God, is driving these nations out of your way. You, however, must be altogether sincere toward the Lord, your God. Though these nations whom you are to dispossess listen to their soothsayers and fortune-tellers, the Lord your

God will not permit you to do so." The Lord God also says in Leviticus 19:31, "Do not go to mediums or consult fortune tellers for you will be defiled by them." Involvement with occultism is a major hindrance to healing. As a matter of fact, this will cause one to be in bondage to the evil one. A person has to renounce this sin, and to invite Jesus to come into his life and to deliver him from the hands of the enemy. A prayer for deliverance may still be needed after he repents and renounces this sin, and opens his heart and welcomes Jesus as his Savior and Healer, and Lord into his life.

For Roman Catholics, the Sacraments of Reconciliation and the Eucharist can help a great deal in casting out the evil spirits from their lives.

7. **Seeking Healing but not the Healer:** This for sure, is a stumbling block to healing. The Healer of course is Jesus Christ. In Isaiah 53:5, the Word of God says, "But He was pierced for our offenses, crushed for our sins, upon Him was the chastisement that makes us whole, by His stripes we were healed." The Word

of God states in Exodus 15:26, "I am the God, your Healer." In Matthew 6:33, Jesus says, "But seek first the Kingdom of God and His righteousness, and all these things will be given you besides."

We have to focus our heart and mind and our entire being on the Lord Jesus Christ and His Lordship over us and not just on the healing of our sickness and pain and suffering.

In 1 Thessalonians 5:16-18, St. Paul says, "Rejoice always. Pray without ceasing. In all circumstances give thanks, for this is the will of God for you in Christ Jesus."

In Luke 17:11-19, we read about the one leper out of the ten who was truly healed because he focused his eyes not on his healing but rather on the Lord Jesus Christ. "As He continued His journey to Jerusalem, He traveled through Samaria and Galilee. As he was entering a village, ten lepers met him. They stood at a distance from Him and raised their voice, saying, "Jesus, Master! Have pity on us!" And when He saw them, He said, "Go show yourselves to the priests." As they were going they were cleansed. And one of them, realizing he had been healed, returned, glorifying God in a loud voice; and he fell at the feet of Jesus and thanked him. He was a Samaritan. Jesus said in reply, "Ten were cleansed, were they not? Where are the other nine? Has none but this foreigner returned to give thanks to God?" Then he said to him, "Stand up and go; your faith has saved you."

8. *Generational Curse*: In Exodus 20:5, the Lord God says, "You shall not bow down to idols nor serve them. For I, the Lord your God, am a jealous God, inflicting punishment for their fathers' wickedness on the children of those who hate me, down to the third and fourth generation." Unless generational curses are broken in Jesus' Name, chances are the sick don't get healed. In Galatians 3:13, St. Paul says, "Christ has redeemed us from the curse of the law, having become a curse for us."

9. *Demonic Attacks*: Demonic spirits not only cause sickness but they could also be a big hindrance to healing. In Luke 9:1, we read, "Then Jesus called His twelve disciples

together and gave them power and authority over all demons, and to cure diseases."

If we sense some demonic presence in
the sick person, a prayer for healing is
not enough, but deliverance prayer may
also be necessary. Sometimes, deliverance from demonic oppression is needed
before the sick can receive physical healing. For instance, we may have to rebuke
and cast out spirits of infirmity and
affliction, spirit of heaviness and bondage, spirit of lust, deaf and dumb spirit,
spirit of demonic oppression, familiar
spirit, familial spirit, spirit of blindness,
and so on in the mighty Name and blood
of Jesus through the mantle of Mary, the
Immaculate Conception, and through
the ministry of the Archangels and
legions of angels.

10. *Lack of Persistence and Perseverance
in Praying for Healing*: Sometimes the
sick will not get their healing because
of lack of perseverance and persistence
in prayer. In Luke 18:1, God's Word
says, "Then Jesus told them a par-
able about the necessity for them to
pray always without becoming weary."

In Luke 11:5-8, "And Jesus said to them, "Suppose one of you has a friend to whom He goes at midnight and says, "Friend, lend me three loaves of bread, for a friend of mine has arrived at my house from a journey and I have nothing to offer him, and he says in reply from within, "Do not bother me; the door has already been locked and my children and I are already in bed. I cannot get up to give you anything. I tell you, if he does not get up to give him the loaves because of their friendship, he will get up to give him whatever he needs because of his persistence." In other words, we should not give up but keep on praying and thanking God. Someone once said that we should use the PUSH method (Pray Until Something Happens).

11. ***Lack of Knowledge or Ignorance of God's Words:*** Sometimes we don't receive the Lord's blessings of healing because we don't know what belongs to us and what our inheritance from the Lord is. In Hosea 4:6-7, the Lord God says, "My people perish for lack of knowledge! Since you have rejected knowledge, I will reject you from my

priesthood; since you have ignored the law of your God, I will also ignore your sons. One and all they sin against me, exchanging their glory for shame."

In Proverbs 4:20-22, God says, "My son, to my words be attentive, to my sayings incline your ear; Let them not slip from your sight, keep them within your heart; For they are life to those who find them, bringing health to one's whole being."

12. ***God's Preeminence and Mystery:*** Sometimes there is no answer to the question of why a person didn't receive his or her healing. In Deuteronomy 29:28, the Word of God says, "The secret things belong to the Lord our God, but those things which are revealed belong to us and to our children forever." We should remember that the things of God cannot always be explained. Our job is to pray for healing and leave the results to the Lord.

13. ***Redemptive Suffering:*** Redemptive suffering is the belief that human suffering, when accepted and offered up in union

with the Passion of Jesus, can remit the just punishment for one's sins or for the sins of another. The Catechism of the Catholic Church #1505 states, "Moved by so much suffering Christ not only allows himself to be touched by the sick, but he makes their miseries his own: "He took our infirmities and bore our diseases." But he did not heal all of the sick. His healings were signs of the coming of the Kingdom of God. They announced a more radical healing—the victory over sin and death through His Passover. On the cross Christ took upon Himself the whole weight of evil and took away the "sin of the world," of which illness is only a consequence. By His passion and death on the cross Christ has given a new meaning to suffering: it can henceforth configure us to Him and unite us with His redemptive Passion.

There are some people who don't receive physical healing or any type of healing for that matter, because the Lord has chosen them to undergo some kind of redemptive suffering which is beneficial for the salvation of their own soul and/ or that of another. Furthermore, I believe that the Lord also gives to those who are being chosen, the strength and the grace to undergo this redemptive suffering. In the Catechism of the Catholic Church #1508, we read "The Holy Spirit gives to some a special charism of healing so as to make manifest the power of the grace of the risen Lord. But even the most intense prayers do not always obtain the healing of all illnesses. Thus St. Paul must learn from the Lord that "my grace is sufficient for you, for my power is made perfect in weakness," and that the sufferings to be endured can mean that "in my flesh I complete what is lacking in Christ's afflictions for the sake of His Body, that is, the Church."

CHAPTER TWELVE

Can I Be a Miracle Worker?

I n John 14:12, Jesus says,

> Amen, amen, I say to you, whoever believes
> in me will do the works that I do, and will
> do greater ones than these, because I'm
> going to the Father.

And what are the works of Jesus? When the disciples of John the Baptist went up to Jesus to ask if He was the Messiah, Jesus replied to them,

> Go and tell John what you have seen and
> heard: the blind regain their sight, the lame
> walk, lepers are cleansed, the deaf hear, the
> dead are raised, the poor have the good news
> proclaimed to them. And blessed is the one
> who takes no offense at me. (Luke 7:22-23)

Can I Be a Miracle Worker?

I've had the opportunities to ask many people during Healing Rallies and crusades in North America, Latin America, South America, Europe, in the Middle East, Africa, Australia, and Asia this question: "How many of you are doing the works of Jesus?" Sad to say, only a handful of Christians claimed that they are doing the works of Jesus. I believe that one of the underlying reasons why signs and wonders, miracles and healings are not being manifested in the lives of many Christians is lack of faith. Many Christians don't believe that the Lord can work with and through them. This unbelief is so closely associated with the feelings of being inadequate and unworthy to be used of and by the Lord.

Jesus says,

> But you will receive power when the Holy Spirit comes upon you, and you will be my witnesses in Jerusalem, throughout Judea and Samaria, and to the ends of the earth. (Acts 1:8)

As baptized believers, our bodies have become temples of the Holy Spirit. We have received that power—the same awesome power that raised Jesus from the dead. Jesus has also given us the authority, or the "power of attorney," to use His precious Name to do His works. In John 14:13-14, Jesus says,

> And whatever you ask in my name, I will do, so that the Father may be glorified in the Son. If you ask anything of me in my name, I will do it.

To do God's works necessitates that we have faith; a faith in the Lord as a Miracle Worker. First, we must have faith in His words and, second, the faith that we can do miracles with and through Him.

Not too long ago, I had the privilege to minister in Daegu, South Korea. There were approximately 9,000 in attendance during the Healing Crusade. The Lord showed the South Koreans that He is still in the healing business. Many in the wheelchairs were able to walk, some blind people started seeing, the deaf started to hear, tumors, cysts, abnormal growths disappeared, and other instantaneous healings took place. "Lord, you sent me to this place to minister to Your people here in Your Mighty Name. Now, Lord, I ask You to back me up. I am powerless, but You are powerful. And nothing is impossible for You. Without You, Lord, I can do nothing, as You know. Let Your Name be glorified by what I say and do here." These were my prayers to Him before I ministered to the people.

To be a miracle worker in the vineyard of the Lord is not difficult at all. An angel said this to Abraham: "Is anything too marvellous for the Lord to do?" (Genesis 18:14) I believe that God's supernatural power is available not only to a few but to all baptized believers. I believe that the Lord is looking for people who are available and willing to be yielded vessels for His resurrection power to flow through them. I believe that He is calling every baptized believer to be a "fool" for Him and to carry out the great commission and to destroy the works of the evil one.

Let us look at some of the ways that we can become effective workers for the Lord.

How to Become an Effective Worker for the Lord

1. ***We have to have Jesus at the center of our lives.*** We should have an intimate, personal relationship with Him. In John 15:4-5, Jesus says, "Remain in me, as I remain in you. Just as a branch cannot bear fruit on its own unless it remains on the vine, so neither can you unless you remain in me. I am the vine, you are the branches. Whoever remains in me and I in him will bear much fruit, because without me you can do nothing."

   We should not only "carry" Jesus with us wherever we go but also we should put Him in front of us, above us, on our side, behind us, and all over us. Then, we should always be ready to "give Him away" to those who are thirsty and hungry for Him. St. Paul says in 2 Corinthians 2:15, "For we are the aroma of Christ for God among those who are being saved and among those who are perishing." Wherever we are, people should not only see Jesus in us, they should be able to smell the "aroma," the "sweet smelling scent" of Jesus in us. Moreover, people around us should be able to "perceive or to get a glimpse" of the Kingdom of Heaven in us.

2. *"Be filled with the Holy Spirit. And do not get drunk on wine, in which lie debauchery, but be filled with the Spirit." (Ephesians 5:18)* Jesus was a Miracle Worker par excellence because He was filled with the Holy Spirit. Not only was He filled by the Spirit but also He was anointed by the Spirit, led by the Spirit, and controlled by the Spirit, and He ministered in the power of the Spirit.

To be filled with the Holy Spirit is to have Jesus in our heart every moment of our lives. In John 7:37-38, we read, "On the last and greatest day of the feast, Jesus stood up and exclaimed, "Let anyone who thirsts come to me and drink. Whoever believes in me, as scripture says: 'Rivers of living water will flow from within Him.'"

The Holy Spirit is our comforter, our sanctifier, our advocate, our teacher, our instructor, and our guide. He is the source of all truth and He also glorifies, reveals, and testifies of Jesus.

3. ***Constant fellowship with the Holy Trinity.*** This can be done through prayer, through listening to His words in our heart, through reading of the Scriptures and most importantly through the reception of the sacraments such as the Sacrament of Reconciliation and the Eucharist. It will help us tremendously, I believe, if we avail ourselves of that "line of communication' between us and the Lord. In 1 Thessalonians 5:17, St. Paul says, "Pray without ceasing." Prayer is not only mouthing off our petitions before the Lord, but prayer should be an avenue for us to listen to His voice. Jesus said that His sheep hear His voice. "The sheep follow Him, because they recognize His voice. As He calls His own sheep by name and leads them out." (John 10:3) The best way, I believe, that we can recognize the voice of the Good Shepherd is by worshipping and fellowshipping with Him on a regular basis.

4. *Always obey the Lord and the promptings of the Holy Spirit.* "If you love me, you will keep my commandments. And I will ask the Father, and he will give you another Advocate to be with you always." (John 14:15-16) When the Holy Spirit prompts me to pray for the paralyzed, the blind, the deaf, or people with incurable diseases, I will not "look" at their circumstances but I will seek the glory of God to be manifested through their healings. To obey the Lord calls us to totally submit ourselves to the Lord and to walk on the "water" with Him. Not too long ago, I was in Lima, Peru, to conduct a Healing Crusade. There was a young lady in her mid twenties who was using a walker. I had a prompting from the Lord to approach her and to pray for her for healing. When asked what she wanted me to pray for her, she told me that she was involved in a car accident and that she was in excruciating pain. She told me further that she could neither stand nor sit for a long time because of the pain. She said her body was stiff from the neck down. As a matter of fact, she had been wearing a neck brace ever since the accident. "My son, speak healing into her body in my Name right now. Tell her that I'm healing her." I heard the Lord speaking into my heart. I obeyed the Lord's promptings right then and there and I laid hands on her. She rested in the Spirit for a while. When she stood up, she was moving her body every which way. She said the pain was totally gone. The following day, she came back and gave her testimony that she got rid of her walker and neck brace because she could already walk normally, as if nothing happened at all. When the Lord ordered me to speak healing into her body, I did not argue with Him nor disobey His words. I did not worry about my reputation or about what people might think or say. I just obeyed His words and did what He asked me to do, and the young lady was healed right there and then. "Now, if you obey me completely and keep my covenant, you will be my treasured possession among all peoples, though all the earth is mine." (Exodus 19:5)

5. ***Ask the Lord to use you mightily for His glory.*** Jesus says, in Matthew 7:7-8, "Ask and it will be given to you; seek and you will find; knock and the door will be

opened to you. For everyone who asks, receives; and the one who seeks, finds; and to the one who knocks, the door will be opened. In Exodus 33:18-19, the Word of God declares, "Then Moses said, "Please let me see your glory!" The LORD answered: "I will make all my goodness pass before you, and I will proclaim my name, 'LORD,' before you; I who show favor to whom I will, I who grant mercy to whom I will." When you ask Him from your heart to use you for His greater glory and honor, be ready and be available because He is always ready when you are, "for the kingdom of God is not a matter of talk but of power." (1 Corinthians 4:20) The Lord is more than willing to use anyone to further His kingdom. Jesus says in Luke 11:13, "If you then, who are wicked, know how to give good gifts to your children, how much more will the Father in heaven give the Holy Spirit to those who ask him?" Can you or I be a miracle worker? I believe the resounding answer to this question is "Yes, we can!" In Ephesians 4:13, St. Paul says, "I have the strength for everything through Him who empowers me."

Inside St. Peter's Basilica in the Vatican in 2014

CHAPTER THIRTEEN

Miraculous Healings of Cancer, Tumors, and Cysts

Then He returned to Cana in Galilee, where He had made the water wine. Now there was a royal official whose son was ill in Capernaum. When he heard that Jesus had arrived in Galilee from Judea, he went to Him and asked Him to come down and heal his son, who was near death. Jesus said to him, "Unless you people see signs and wonders, you will not believe." The royal official said to him, "Sir, come down before my child dies." Jesus said to him, "You may go; your son will live." The man believed what Jesus said to him and left. While he was on his way back, his slaves met him and told him that his boy would live. He asked them when he began to recover. They told him, "The fever left him yesterday, about one in the afternoon." The father realized that just at that time Jesus had said to him, "Your son will live," and he and his whole household came to believe." (John 4:46-53)

Jesus is the Divine Healer. He heals in total obedience to his Heavenly Father. In John 5:19-20, Jesus says, "Amen, amen, I say to you, a son cannot do anything on his own, but only what his Father is doing; for what he does, his son will do also. For the Father loves his Son and shows Him everything that he himself does, and He will show Him greater works than these, so that you may be amazed."

The following testimonies of healings demonstrate the healing and loving touch of the Lord Jesus.

"I want to give a testimony on behalf of my six-year-old daughter, Katie. She was diagnosed with Stage 4 neuroblastoma cancer in March 2013. Bob Canton prayed over her twice—once over the phone and again during the Alliance of Filipino Catholic Charismatic Prayer Communities' National Convention in Burbank. Many wonderful things happened to her. Although she did not get instant healing, our journey was met with lots of encouraging news, and the final one was she is cancer free as of June 2014. I have also started going to prayer group and during one of

the sessions, a member with the gift of words of knowledge revealed that Jesus has healed my daughter, and we are to follow the instruction of the doctors. Since then I knew my daughter will be okay. Every time we encountered difficulties/complications, we overcame them without any consequences. Few examples are when my daughter had to have surgical removal of her tumor, the doctor had to do a huge incision from the side of her chest to the back and had to cut through ribs!

In recovery she did not suffer any pain and was discharged in three days without any pain meds! Praise God. During the transplant, she was diagnosed with thrombotic microangiopathy with high blood pressure, which is a potentially disastrous diagnosis and could become chronic. She was discharged with complete recovery and no blood pressure medications. During immunotherapy, she started to develop allergic reactions with hives and visual changes, which could potentially worsen and mean we could not get treatment anymore. Through prayers with Bob Canton and my family, the next day she completely recovered. Now she is back to her old self. We completed all the treatment per orders from the doctors. She was initially given a 10-20 percent chance of survival. Now I know she is in 100 percent survival. Praise God. I thank the Lord for using Bob Canton as His instrument. Most of all, I thank God for healing my daughter completely. Our God is a God of miracles."

—*Irene Toh, Los Angeles, CA*—

"It is with profound thanksgiving to God that I write this letter of testimony. On Saturday, February 18, 1995, I attended the Mass and Healing service here at St. Luke's parish. This testimony is written one month to the day.

Bob Canton received a word of knowledge that the Lord Jesus through the power of the Holy Spirit was healing people with tumors, cancers, cysts, and abnormal growths. I had cysts in both of my breasts. I raised my hand to claim the healing. Thereafter, he prayed over me for the fullness of healing. The following week, I began to feel aching discomfort in the areas of my cysts and by the weekend, the ache and the cysts were gone. Exactly a month later, my doctor, E. Lewis Cobb, M.D. F.A.C.O.G, gave me a medical examination to confirm the healing. His words were 'great, terrific, wonderful!' as he examined me and could no longer palpate any abnormalities in my breasts. It was a very joyful experience to witness God's healing and to share it with a medical doctor. In his quiet, gentle way, Dr. Cobb readily wrote out the enclosed diagnosis. The healing has brought me great joy and I hope it will help others seek and find the healing power of Jesus. I would also like to thank the members of the Children of God Prayer Community of St. Luke's for their faithfulness in serving the Lord Jesus.

—*Mary Hummel, Stockton, CA*—

"Examined patient Mary Hummel on March 16, 1995, and no abnormality of breast noticed. Previous cysts not palpated."
—*E. Lewis Cobb, M.D.*—

"My mother Helen Hummel who lives in Kansas City, Missouri, had her breast and about thirty-seven lymph nodes removed from her right side, as they had cancer in them. She received chemotherapy and radiation treatments. After a few years, they discontinued both treatments, since the cancer seemed to have spread through her body and the treatments did not seem to be working. Later on, I was called back to Kansas City because mom was in the hospital with blood clots in her lungs. The doctors told my sister to call for the family, as mom would not live long. She made it through the next critical days and was released. Her doctor gave her six months to live. She was assigned a hospice care representative and given morphine and oxygen at home. She had gotten progressively weaker as her cancer spread. Her morphine had to be increased to continue to work on her pain. Three months later, Mary and I attended the Children of God Prayer Community's Healing Mass to pray for my neck injury. During the Healing Service, Mary began to experience discomfort in her right hip and extreme discomfort in her left leg and hip. Thinking it was her varicose veins or the hard chairs or the combination of the two, she tried to make herself as comfortable as possible. Mary stood in proxy for mom to

be prayed over by the healing team headed by Bob Canton. A few weeks later, Mary again stood proxy for my mother at the Children of God Prayer Community's Healing Service. Over the next two to three weeks, Mary experienced discomfort high in her left breast, right lymph nodes, and hips. Mary wrote to my mother, explained the phenomenon of "proxy pain," and suggested that her cancer may be cured. On May 18, we found that my mother had gone back to her doctor for tests. When he called her for the results, he said, 'I don't understand it, we must have misdiagnosed you. I cannot find any sign of cancer in your body.' He then began the difficult transition of reducing the morphine in or order to completely take mom off the drug. She is regaining her strength, walking more, and pushing her wheelchair instead of riding! We praise God in His mercy, and we thank Him for answering our prayers!"
—Frank and Mary Hummel, Stockton, CA—

The following testimony from Florida Cowan of Las Vegas, Nevada, shows that the healing touch of the Lord Jesus has no limits.

"I was diagnosed three years ago with a tumor in my throat. My doctor had recommended for me to undergo surgery. Because I didn't have enough insurance coverage, I opted to forgo the surgery. I knew of Bob Canton's healing ministry through Dr. Linda Carder who is a very close friend of mine. One evening I called Bob because the tumor was bothering me. Bob then prayed with me

over the telephone. I felt heat and tingling sensations as we prayed. He told me that healings were in progress. He prayed with me again on three other occasions within a period of six weeks, and he told me every time we prayed to thank and praise the Lord Jesus Christ who is the Divine Healer. I recently went to see my doctor for more tests and examinations. The test results showed that the tumor had disappeared. When I heard this good news from my doctor, I couldn't help but praise God the Father, His Son Jesus, and the Holy Spirit. I know God loves me very much. Now I constantly turn to Him and I aspire to grow in holiness in accordance to His will."

—*Florida Cowan, Las Vegas, NV*—

The following testimony is from Walter Grotecke, who resides in Clearwater, Florida. Indeed, for God, nothing is impossible at all.

"Three years ago we invited Bob Canton back to Tampa Bay. We had a healing service in a Clearwater church. A girlfriend's father, Richard, who had terminal colon cancer attended. Bob prayed over Richard and made the sign of the Cross on his forehead. Richard fell into my arms cancer free to this day.

Four years ago, a close friend told my wife that her father, Herbert, was diagnosed with terminal lung cancer. The doctors gave him a couple of months to live. I sent an e-mail to Bob to pray for our friend's father. Bob did.

Herbert is alive to this day without lung cancer."
—Walter Grotecke, Clearwater, FL—

"I'd heard of healings in the Bible, but I never imagined one would happen to me. In 2008, I had aggressive Stage 3 breast cancer. After surgeries, chemotherapy, and radiation, I was struck with lymphedema—a significant swelling of my left arm, hand, and fingers—that is permanent. No cure. My arm was also numb and had limited range of motion. I met Bob Canton in 2009, at a Festival of Healing and Worship Conference in Arizona. Brother Bob prayed over me and said, 'Sister, great things will be happening for you.' I also received a copy of Bob's Healing and Keeping Prayer and prayed it with expectant faith daily for almost two years, while also seeking God through women's Bible study, Mass, prayer groups, retreats (Christ Renews His Parish and a Cursillo), and Charismatic Renewal. On September 23, 2011, in my kitchen a "voice" spoke to my heart stating, 'You are healed.' And my arm was instantly restored to normal. My doctors said it is "medically unexplainable." At my five-year cancer checkup recently, my oncologist declared, 'Frankly, I'm surprised you're still alive. Whatever you are doing, keep on doing it.' He also affirmed me cancer-free. With God, all things are possible. Have faith!"
—Mary Erin O'Brien, Mesa, AZ—

My name is Xiomara Lopez. I live here in Masaya, Nicaragua. Almost a year ago, someone gave me your Healing and Keeping Prayer. I thank God for this prayer because it is marvelous. I say this prayer daily with great fervor. I am a practicing Catholic. I am writing to you to let you know of my testimony to the wonders that the Heavenly Father has done to my daughter and to our family. Approximately four months ago, my daughter was diagnosed by her doctor to have a cervical cancer.

Everybody in our family and some of our friends started praying for my daughter using the Healing and Keeping Prayer every day. We prayed and prayed for my daughter. Two months ago, her doctor did a biopsy on her. The result was unbelievable. The doctor said that the cancerous cells disappeared completely. They could not find any cancerous cell.

The Lord listened to our prayers and He freed my daughter from a very cruel and deadly illness. The Lord once more heard our prayers. Thank you, Lord, thank you, Lord. We made many copies of the Healing and Keeping Prayer and we gave them to many of our relatives and friends, including our parish priest. Thank you for writing and for distributing this prayer everywhere in the world.

—Xiomara Lopez, Masaya, Nicaragua—

"I had a big lump or cyst in my throat for ten years and I had difficulty eating solid foods. It was very hard for

me but all these inconveniences I offered to the Lord Jesus daily in my prayers, and I had accepted this suffering.

I was invited by my son Ramon and his wife Cirila to attend the Healing and Miracle Service conducted by Bob Canton at Our Lady of Rule Church in Lapu-lapu City, Mactan, Philippines. During the Miracle Service, Bob asked those present who have been suffering from sinusitis to come forward for prayers. I came forward for prayers, and I experienced what Bob calls resting in the Spirit. Then, after a while, Bob said that he had sensed the Lord healing those who have cysts, or lumps, or tumors. I stayed and I was again prayed over and rested in the Spirit for the second time. Then I touched my throat and I found out that the cyst was gone. The miracle of all miracles happened, because the Lord Jesus Christ healed me instantly and completely. I gave witness to this blessing to the huge crowd, which attended the Miracle Service. The Lord has been good to me in spite of all my sins. And I give glory and praise to the King of Kings. I will bless the Lord Jesus all the days of my life."

—*Concepcion Jayme, Cebu City, Philippines*—

"Bob, thank you for praying with my daughter and with all of us in Miami. You came to speak during the Shalom Festival here in Miami, and we took the opportunity to come to you and asked for your prayers. Last August 2013, after her biopsy, my daughter Alexis was diagnosed as having thyroid cancer. They found cancerous tissues and

abnormal bleeding. Yesterday was the second biopsy for my daughter for her thyroid so the doctors could decide whether to do the surgery or to proceed with the chemotherapy treatment. After reading the results of the tests and biopsy, the doctor just could not believe it because this time they found nothing; everything was normal. The doctor had to check my daughter's ID to make sure that she was the same person that they saw last August. She asked my daughter, 'What happened, what did you do?' We remember that after you prayed with her, you told us that we would be getting good reports from her doctors. You told us not to worry, but to keep on praying for her. So this is the good report that you were talking about. It's Jesus. The Lord heard our prayers. Jesus, we praise and thank you. Our daughter's faith in the Lord has gone sky-high. Our faith in Jesus has really increased. Thank you so much for taking the time to pray with my daughter and with all of us. It has changed darkness around us into God's light."
—Joe, Valsamma, and Alexis, Miami, FL—

"Ever in awe of God's power and grace, I have written to share a story of His love—a love I've always known but have never fully understood and felt until now. I've suffered from abdominal pains for years. The medical diagnosis was ulcer. The dramatic decline of my health began. I had fever, unusual tiredness, loss of appetite, nausea, vomiting, itchiness, sleeplessness, depression, serious weight loss, and jaundice, the yellowing of the eye and skin. A liver profile

test pointed to hepatitis but showed negative after a series of more blood tests and prayers. At the recommendation of a specialist, an abdominal and pelvic CT scan was done. The radiology report came—letters and words read to me that would changed my life forever.

Carcinoma of the pancreas was the medical term used. They found a malignant tumor within the head of the pancreas. A radically complicated $150,000 surgery was proposed but promised nothing. Having been only twenty-seven years of age, my mom and dad were beyond shocked to learn I had cancer. They summoned up all their courage and tried to talk to me with the utmost optimism, even though I knew they were torn apart inside. I wept for my family who obviously loved me and embraced me with all their prayers. One of them was my Aunt Nenette S. Catbagan, who asked you, Bob, to pray for me and to pray with me over the phone. The longest few hours of my life then followed. Only prayers held me from plunging into the murkiest, deepest chasms of sadness, loneliness, and despair. Four months later, a miracle was announced. The head radiologist and the gastroenterologist who was to perform the operation declared that there was now no tumor to be found. An ERCP confirmed the absence of pancreatic cancer. A gall stone blocking the bile duct was deemed the culprit instead and was easily remedied by a non-surgical procedure called papillotomy. I have fully recovered both physically and spiritually and mentally.

When science had what it had to offer, all I really needed to heal was the Lord Jesus, the prayers, especially yours Bob, and my new-found self whose heart was truly opened up,

allowing Him in and letting His glorious presence lead the
way. I am eternally grateful. Praise be to God!"
—George L. Yasis, Oakdale, MN—

"Thank you for praying for my Dad's healing and deliv-
erance from lung cancer. The following is our testimony of
God's miraculous healing power.

My Dad, Larry Ecker, received a Goliath of a diagnosis
on April 13, 2012—Stage 4 Adenocarcinoma lung can-
cer metastasized to spine and a few bones. This diagnosis
was very surprising as Dad, a non-smoker, did not have
any symptoms except for back pain. The spinal tumor had
fractured two vertebrae, which required surgery. Due to
the back pain, Dad was on pain medication every four
hours. Sitting in a chair or walking became very difficult.
Bending over was nearly impossible.

The words from the Lord that you shared with my dad
at the beginning of this journey of healing were: 'Do not
despair, do not despair, do not let this enemy come against
you. Know that in me, there is victory, victory, victory. Hang
on to me.'

We took Dad to Mayo Clinic in Rochester, Minnesota,
for radiation and chemotherapy. Dad had five radiation
treatments during the first week of May 2012. After the
second treatment, instead of pushing Dad in a wheelchair
to the radiation room, I was pushing the wheelchair full
of our belongings and trying to keep up with Dad as he
walked quickly to the radiation room. After the radiation

treatments were completed, Dad asked the radiation oncologist if he would be able to drive his tractor again. The radiation oncologist was very cautious with his reply, sharing the news that the spinal tumor was within 1-2 millimeters of the spinal cord.

Before Dad started his first round of chemotherapy on May 24, 2012, you shared the following words from the Lord: 'My son, let not your heart be troubled, I am with you and you'll be amazed at what I will do.'

By May 28, Dad no longer needed the pain medication and was back driving his tractor in the fields. Dad continued his chemotherapy treatments at Mayo Clinic during the summer. He did extremely well with the treatments, often eating Mexican food the next day after a treatment. He continued to work in the fields throughout the summer. We were shouting praises to God when on July 26, 2012, the CT scan showed a 40 percent reduction of the lung tumor.

On October 4, 2012, Dad was scheduled for a CT scan. I received the words from the Lord in the early morning hours, 'Do not be disappointed.' I was puzzled because we all expected a good report since the last CT scan indicated a 40-percent tumor reduction. We met with the medical oncologist after the CT scan and received the news that the lung tumor had returned to its original size, which indicated the cancer was aggressive and his particular chemo was no longer effective. Prior to our departure for Mayo Clinic, my brother had received the following words from the Lord 'Do not believe the report.' He was afraid to share it with us as we were all expecting a good report. Now the words from the Lord made sense.

Dad started a new chemotherapy drug in mid-October. *The side effects were more challenging; however, Dad continued to persevere with the Lord's strength and grace. A CT scan on November 28 indicated the lung tumor remained the same size, which was great news. Dad continued his treatments even though it was rough. A February 4, 2013, CT scan indicated the lung tumor continued to show no signs of growth; another good report! During this appointment with the medical oncologist, he recommended a clinical study for Dad, which would require tissue from the lung tumor. Since there was not enough tumor tissue left over from the May 2012 lung tumor biopsy, surgery was scheduled for March 5.*

On March 5, 2013, a Mayo Clinic surgeon inserted a scope into Dad's lungs to take photographs of the tumor and to remove some tissue for the clinical study. The surgeon told us that he was unable to obtain any tissue due to lack of tumor burden. He scoped the entire lung—all clear—and lymph glands were clear. The tumor had become scar tissue. He said without the camera to confirm the tumor had become scar tissue, future CT scans would show the scar tissue as the tumor! All praise to God! The next day, the medical oncologist said to my Dad, 'I continue to be amazed with you.' Those words reminded me of the words Bob had received on May 24, 2012, that we would be amazed at what the Lord would do. Indeed, we were. The Lord had turned the tumor into scar tissue.

Dad returned to Mayo Clinic on April 4, 2013, for a P.E.T. scan. We received the results: 'There is no visual evidence of active cancer in your body.' The lung tumor, spinal tumor, and cancerous spots on other bones were gone! It is truly a miracle, and we praise God and give Him the glory.

Thank you, Bob, for all your prayers and for standing with us during this journey of healing. The words you received from the Lord provided direction, comfort, and peace. Yes, we found victory, victory, victory in the Lord, and we continue to be amazed at what the Lord has done!"

—Cindy Scheublein, Stockton, CA—

"In July 2009, I had a biopsy. The doctor told my wife and family that most likely it was cancer. It would take a week for results. This really concerned us, because nine years earlier I was diagnosed with colon cancer and by the Grace of God and three surgeries later, I was healed from the cancer. As days went by, we had many sleepless nights. When we went to get the results, we had strength and peace and comfort due to the prayer support of family and friends, including Bob Canton, whose message from God was, 'Be not afraid for I go before you. Your healing is underway for my Father's glory.' When the Doctor came in, he smiled and said you're okay—no cancer. He then said he didn't understand it. From what he saw, it was cancer. He even had it tested three different ways to make sure. My wife told him it was by the Grace of God that the cancer was gone. He said, 'I guess so; there's no other explanation.'

He was happy to give good news. We give all honor and glory to God for His healing touch and for Bob who was very understanding with us even when we called him late at night at various times for prayer."
—*Ralph Ontiveros, Stockton, CA*—

"I have not attended any Healing Rally. However, I have been saying your Healing and Keeping Prayer daily since my CT scan showed three nodules in my abdomen seven months ago. They were discovered after I had completed my surgery and radiation therapy for cancer of the cervix. My husband also stood in for me during the Healing Rally conducted by you at the Church of the Risen Christ in Singapore.

Another CT scan was performed recently after I had completed two cycles of chemotherapy and undergone an emergency operation for acute intestinal obstruction. The recent CT scan shows that there is no lump present in my abdomen or any of my other major organs.

I want to thank God, our loving and merciful Father, for his divine healing, blessings, ceaseless love, and unfailing support for me during this most difficult and stressful time of my life. He is a living God in my life. Praise the Lord!"
—*Frances K., Singapore*—

"My name is Ann. I used to live in Chicago but moved to New Hampshire a year ago. To start with, in March of 2010, I had a good-sized lump on my right breast. I panicked and I could say that I was really worried and full of anguish. Night and day I cried out to God and I could not help it. My husband sent you an e-mail just trying his luck if you would answer him. He wrote you about my situation. To our surprise, in God's glory, you answered his e-mail. You started praying for me as you stated in your e-mail.

I had my series of checkups, mammogram, ultrasound, and MRI. The night before my checkups, we called you at 11:00 P.M. (Chicago time) since you told us to call you so you could pray over me by phone. But we only got your voicemail. That made me worry a lot because I was convinced I could not sleep that night without your prayers. We left a message for you to call us anytime of the day or night. As you could see, we were desperate for your call and prayers for me. At 2:00 A.M., our phone rang and it was you, Brother Bob. I was really excited when you called. You told us you just came home from overseas ministering to thousands of people in South Korea. After you prayed over me, I was relieved. The following day, my husband and I went to Lutheran Hospital for my series of checkups. A few days later, I received a phone call from my doctor's office telling me that they didn't find any malignancy or any abnormalities in my breast and that everything was OK. By the way, the lump also disappeared after you prayed with me on the phone. It was a miracle for me. My son was jumping up and down with happiness after we heard the results from my doctor. God is so good that He sent you to us. You sent us a copy of the Healing and Keeping Prayer, and we are praying that prayer every day. We're able to memorize it (me, my husband, and my son) and sent copies to our relatives and friends not only in Chicago and in New Hampshire but also in the Philippines. Right after I received the results from my doctor, if you could still remember, my husband sent you a letter, thanking you for everything you did for us. My family is very thankful to God for answering all our prayers. We are so grateful we knew you as God's instrument for healing. Thank you for giving us your precious time to pray with us.

More power to you and, remember, you are in our prayers always."

—*Ann, Frankie and Andre, NH*—

Prayer for Healing of Cancer, Tumors, and Cysts

Father in heaven, thank you for loving me and for sending your only beloved son, Jesus Christ, to be my Savior and my Healer. Lord Jesus Christ, I praise your most holy and mighty Name.

Have mercy on me, and forgive me for the sins that I have committed and for all the things that I failed to do to glorify your holy Name. Cover me Lord with your precious blood from the top of my head to the soles of my feet. I apply by faith your precious blood, the same blood that you shed on the Cross on Calvary according to Isaiah 53, directly into all my cells and tissues, all my organs, my bones, my blood vessels and veins, and into all the systems of my body. I command my immunity system to produce a powerful "blast" to destroy and obliterate all the cancerous cells in my body in Jesus Name. I command all my killer cells, the B cells and the T cells, to eat out all the cancerous cells and I speak life and restoration into all my cells, my organs, my systems, my bones, and my tissues in my entire body in Jesus Name, and by the power of the Holy Spirit. In Jesus name and by the power of Jesus' blood, I command all infirmities and sickness and weaknesses and fear, and heaviness, bondages, and anxieties to leave my body, mind, and spirit, and I command the chemical, electrical, and physical frequencies in my body to be in balance and in harmony. In Jesus Name, I take authority over all forms of tumors, cancerous and abnormal growths, and cysts, and I command them to disappear and to leave my body completely and go to the foot of the Cross of Jesus and I forbid them from coming back.

I break and cancel out and declare null and void all curses, spells, evil wishes, evil desires, evil pronouncements, evil works against me and my body in the name and by the blood of Jesus. I command all the medications that I am taking to be very effective in treating me without any ill effects or complications in my body, in Jesus Name and by the power of the Holy Spirit. Lord Jesus, I give you permission to do what is best for me. Renew me physically, emotionally, mentally, spiritually, and psychologically, through the power of your love. Fill me with your Holy Spirit and help me become more like you every moment of my life. Let your joy and peace and wholeness be upon me always. I put a seal over all my body with the precious name and blood of Jesus by faith so that I can keep all my healings.

Lord, may you be glorified through my healings. I ask this in Jesus' Name through the mantle of Mary, the Immaculate Conception, Amen.

Meeting with His Holiness Pope Benedict XV1 in 2011, now
Pope Emeritus Benedict XV1.

CHAPTER FOURTEEN

Miraculous Healings of Blindness and Other Eye Diseases

In Matthew 20:29-34, we read,

As Jesus and His disciples were leaving Jericho, a large crowd followed him. Two blind men were sitting by the roadside, and when they heard that Jesus was going by, they shouted, "Lord, Son of David, have mercy on us!"

The crowd rebuked them and told them to be quiet, but they shouted all the louder, "Lord, Son of David, have mercy on us!"

Jesus stopped and called them. "What do you want me to do for you?" He asked. "Lord," they answered, "we want our sight."

Jesus had compassion on them and touched their eyes. Immediately they received their sight and followed Him.

In many Healing Crusades and Healing Services that I have had the privilege to conduct, I have witnessed blind people made able to see again. Yes, Jesus is still in the business of healing blind eyes. I even have collections of eyeglasses from people who do not have the need to use them again.

Not too long ago, I was in Teresina, in the State of Piaui, Brazil, to conduct a Healing Crusade. A nineteen-year-old man named Danny, who was blind since birth, regained his sight after I prayed with him for healing in Jesus' Name. It was a tremendous blessing for me to witness so many healings and to see many people either on their knees or dancing around with great enthusiasm, hands raised up high, tears on the cheeks praising and thanking the Lord for the miracles that they were receiving and witnessing in their midst. The atmosphere in the place was electric. Yes, indeed, the Master Healer is still in the healing business. Here are some accounts of His mighty deeds in the New Testament. "Moving on from there, Jesus walked by the Sea of Galilee, went up on the mountain, and sat down there. Great crowds came to him, having with them the lame, the blind, the deformed, the mute, and many others. They placed them at his feet, and he cured them. The crowds were amazed when they saw the mute speaking, the deformed made whole, the lame walking, and the blind able to see, and they glorified the God of Israel." (Matthew 15:29-31)

"Jesus went around to all the towns and villages, teaching in their synagogues, proclaiming the Gospel of the kingdom, and curing every disease and illness. At the sight of the crowds, His heart was moved with pity for them because they were troubled and abandoned, like sheep without a shepherd. Then he said to his disciples, 'The harvest is abundant but the laborers are few; so ask the master of the harvest to send out laborers for his harvest.'" (Matthew 9:35-38)

The following are some of the testimonies that I have received from those who have been healed of their blindness and other eye diseases.

Once I was blind, but now I see. A grateful Mary, whose central vision just got restored.

"Ten years ago I was writing, and my hand got stiff and I could not see out of my left eye. The doctors at the Cleveland Clinic diagnosed it as "central vein occlusion." Five years later, it happened again, this time in the other eye. The doctors also diagnosed it as, "central vein occlusion." This condition resulted in my inability to see. Everything became a blur. Color perception was gone, and I could no longer read, drive, and see faces. I "read" through tapes and listened to the news on TV without seeing.

Today, after the Healing Workshop and after Bob Canton prayed over me, I noticed I could see faces. I could see

the face of Brother Bob. I could see the color of his necktie. I got so excited. I wanted to go home right away because I could not wait to see the face of my grandchild."
—Mary Anderson, Columbus, OH—

"I had been on medication for glaucoma for almost two years. The doctor put me on some medicine that helped my eye pressure go low. If my eye pressure had gone too high, I could have lost my eyesight. My doctor told me that I would be on that medicine for a lifetime. Every night I had to put eye drops in each eye, hoping that the pressure would go down. My eye doctor had to see me every four weeks. Each visit, he would ask, 'Are you taking this medicine every night? Your pressure did not go down very much, so I will switch you to another medicine.' I then took another medicine. Still, my eye doctor was not really happy with the results. My mother suggested that I should get prayed over by my uncle, Bob Canton. To tell the truth, I did not feel like I deserved to get prayed over because I just felt so guilty of the sins I had committed and was scared to ask God to heal my eyes. Weeks passed, and my mom continued to urge me to get prayed over. One day, Uncle Bob came to use my computer. My mom quickly asked him to pray over my eyes. I felt kind of uneasy about this because I was scared to come forth to the Lord. After my uncle prayed over me, I felt better, somehow. I felt like God was there with me.

A few days passed and I had to go see another eye doctor. He did some tests. I waited in the room, feeling very nervous and anxious. I prayed a quick prayer to God. Finally, the doctor came in with my tests and said, 'This is outstanding. You passed the test! You do not have glaucoma. This is incredible.' I smiled so hard. The eye doctor told me that I needed to see Dr. Wong, the glaucoma specialist, to see if I still needed to take the medicine for my eyes. Passing the glaucoma test made me cry. That showed me how much God loves me and still listens to me even though I had committed so many sins. There I was, feeling so guilty and not wanting to get prayed over, but then God still came along with His touch for me!

On the way home, I just kept crying. Praise God; He does so many wonders, and it is so amazing! And one more thing: Dr. Wong told me that I do not have to take the medicine for my eyes. Imagine that! I was supposed to take that medication for a lifetime, and now I am off it! This is all because of the Lord! God has touched me.

To those out there who are afraid to speak with God, do not be afraid. This miracle has taught me that God is there for you no matter what. The Lord is so good and that is so wonderful! We should always praise the Lord. He does so many wonders. Thank You Jesus!"

—Miriam Canton Al-sayegh—

"My daughter, Chelsea, was born clinically blind on her right eye. It is a one-in-a-million case according to the specialists of UCLA's Eye Institute. The diagnosis was tissue hyperplasia vitreous. A tissue that was supposed to dissolve between the retina and the lens while in the womb did not dissolve. That caused the lazy eye movement and also no vision. It was discovered later, when Chelsea was ten months old, that the tissue had already hardened and it was no longer possible to do surgery because the procedure could have further damaged the lens and the retina. The eye specialists said that a human being can live for 150 years with only one eye working. For the last eleven years, Chelsea had only one eye working.

A miracle happened on the ninth day of March when we attended your healing service at Our Lady of Las Vegas. After you prayed over Chelsea, she was slain by the Spirit. She was touched by the Holy Spirit and cried. When you tested her vision, I was surprised that she was able to follow your hand movement with her left eye being covered. I'd been attending prayer healings, but this was more dramatic and real. God waited for this moment of her age to heal her right eye so that young people and all people will know that Jesus is alive by the power of His Holy Spirit.

As a family, we will continue to pray for complete healing of our souls, for daily conversion, and to serve the Lord. Praise the Lord! Alleluia! Hail Mary!"

—*Cecil, Helen, Chelsea, and Ben Andre, Las Vegas, NV*—

"I had lost a great deal of sight in my left eye due to glaucoma. Because glaucoma is incurable and surgery was done to prevent further loss, and the Doctor at UC Davis had me undergo an MRI of the brain and optic nerve, naturally I was so afraid. Some good friends from St. Luke's Parish said I should go to the Healing Mass. Their faith is so strong, and they told me that many people had been healed through your ministry. So, in September, I attended the Healing Mass. You and your team prayed over me.

It is hard to explain the experience of total surrender to God; it is a feeling of complete peace and trust, which for me in itself is a miracle. I know from just that experience that God was teaching me: we do not just see with our eyes; we see through our emotions, our fears, and the baggage of past experiences. We see through our souls. Without trust in God, we cannot say confidently: 'I believe, I love, I adore, I hope.' That is what God wanted me to learn in that healing.

Secondly, I received a call from UC Davis that the results of the MRI were: no abnormalities, no lesions; and it would not be necessary to follow up with the neuro-ophthalmologist. Thank God! My eyes have really improved a lot ever since that day you prayed over me, and new glasses will improve my vision even more. I trust in God's power and goodness. I know now, fear is not faith. Thank you, Bob Canton, and your healing teams for bringing God's Love and healing to us.

Sometimes I think, well, there is a "horse whisperer" to calm down unmanageable horses, and a "dog whisperer" to help dogs with all sorts of problems. And so it is that I can call Bob Canton, the "soul whisperer," and I mean that with thanks and respect and I ask God to help you reach out and help as many souls as possible. God bless you and your healing teams. You are a great blessing to those who are sick and in need of God's healing touch."
—Shirley Solari, Stockton, CA—

"I am Wellington Soares, and I'm currently coordinator of Youth Ministry in the Diocese of Campo Maior in the state of Piauí in my beloved Brazil. When you came to preach during the Catholic Charismatic Congress in this state last June, I was there with my prayer group and family, and my wife was Gilvane. Our friend, Alegia, also came and she asked you to pray for her to have a baby. She and her husband wanted to have a baby for a long time. When you prayed for her, I was there. You told her not to worry but to thank God because God hears our prayers. You told her that she would get good news from God. By the grace of God, Alegia is now two months pregnant, and that was two months after you prayed for her. Thank you, thank you for your faith, your mission, and your yes to God. Thank you also to God, for in you God accomplishes his word: 'Verily, verily I say unto you, he who believes in me will also do the works that I do, and will do greater works than these, because I go to the Father' (John 14:12)

Thanks always. God bless you, and our Holy Mother the Virgin Mary always is with you and your works. We hope you come back to Brazil soon. People in Brazil need you. I saw in my own eyes the healing of that nineteen-year-old man who was born blind when you prayed for him and the healing of that blind woman and the woman walking from the wheelchair and many other healings. It was very great. I really believe what you said that Jesus is our Healer."

—*Wellington Soares, State of Piaui, Brazil*—

PS: Alegia does not speak or understand English, so she asked me to write to you. "Thank you."

"I attended a healing retreat hosted by Catholic Charismatic Renewal of New Orleans (CCRNO), in Louisiana, October 11-13, 2013, led by Bob Canton. Due to damage to my joints caused by chemotherapy, I had been walking for a few years with a cane, as I was very prone to falling. Additionally, I had been diagnosed with a family eye disorder, called Stargardt's Disease, a form of macular degeneration. My vision had been steadily declining due to cataracts in both eyes, as well as to the chemo treatments, which I was still receiving. Bob Canton prayed over me, asking that I would be able to walk without the cane and for a strengthening in my ankles and feet. One of my traveling companions told him that I was blind and needed my eyes healed. Bob prayed over me, and then had me start walking around without my

cane. As I walked, I could feel my ankles and feet getting stronger. What I could not explain at that time was why I had a weird feeling in my body. I later prayed and discovered that all of my joints were being healed; shoulders, ribs, arms, etc. Also, my heart felt strange. Since my chemo treatments, I had had some issues with my heart; but since that evening, I have not experienced those same problems. I made a determined effort after Bob prayed over me to not use my cane. I put it in my guest room and left it there for the remainder of that weekend. That was very strange and still can be disconcerting to this day, as I have moments where I want to use it but consciously, do not.

That evening, before our group broke for dinner, Bob returned to me to pray over my eyes. He did, and I could see what he was doing. During dinner, one of my friends noticed that my eyes were able to focus. Up to that point, I had one eye that roamed to the right and the other to the left. They are now focused. The cloudiness of cataracts is gone from both eyes. I revel at how much more light is entering my eyes! Also, I know my eyesight is improving greatly, because I can see things better, even without my glasses. Bob told me that I would have more healing of my eyes over time, and I have found this to be true.

Two additional healings I may have received are for two cancers—CLL and MCL. My future doctor visits may give me an additional opportunity to publicly thank Our Lord for even more blessings. Time will tell. I am so blessed by God for what He has bestowed on me.

I am thanking Him for what He wants me to do with these healings. YEAH, GOD!!!"
   —*Kathleen DePhillips, Birmingham, AL*—

"Tina Sallame is in her early seventies and losing her sight since six years ago. She is diabetic and she has been using a magnifying glass to try to read or see, and she cannot read any letters without the magnifying glass. Every day, the day is foggy and cloudy to her. She cannot see even near. She came to church when she heard Bob Canton was coming to do healing ministry. She is a believer in God and looked forward to going to church. Bob prayed over her. Praise the Lord, she can now see. She can see Father Raymund Ellorin now clearly. Before, when he used to visit her, only with his voice could she tell that he is a man. She said she rejoices and likes what she can see on Father Raymund and the surroundings.

Bob asked if she could see outside the church through the entrance. Tina could see the stop sign, which was about 100 yards away. She could see the police car that was parked in front of the police station and later told Bob that the policeman was going to the police car and moving away. She also could see the palm leaves that were swaying outside the church entrance. She also suffers pains in her feet. She walks with a cane and dolly. She also now feels stronger. Thank God, she has been healed."
   —*Nora E., Lanai, HI*—

"I have been meaning to send you a praise report regarding many healings that I have received from the Lord through your prayers. At last, I found the time to do it before the end of 2013.

I was healed from a painful, disabling back injury from a car crash after you prayed over me, and God healed me completely. To God be the glory. I have witnessed so many people healed miraculously through your prayer interventions. Last time I went to California, I went for an eye checkup. During our rosary at Victoria Fuentez Evans' house, you prayed over me. Two days later, I went to my eye doctor for my follow-up visit, and he was baffled because the astigmatism in my left eye was gone totally. Thank you, Jesus. I am so proud and thankful of you Bob and your ministry and humbled to be part of you prayer community and having served in the prayer group's music ministry. Job well done, Bob.

Please continue to do your beautiful ministry of helping the sick in the name of Jesus. Hope to see you in Cebu City for Healing Crusades soon.

—*Liz Fernandez, Cebu City, Philippines*—

"Be Transformed... What a weekend... the SCRC Convention in Anaheim, California was amazing, good Spirit-filled theme: 'Be Transformed'—taken from Romans 12:1-2, 'I urge you therefore brothers by the mercies of God to offer your bodies as a living sacrifice holy and pleasing to

God your spiritual worship. Do not conform yourselves to this age but be transformed by the renewal of your mind that you may discern what is the will of God what is good and pleasing and perfect.'

All I can say is that God moved with His Spirit and touched many lives this past weekend. People were healed, including me. Praise God! The youth and young adults experienced God's loving mercy and forgiveness like no other. Can't describe how people felt but just knew in my heart that people were at peace.

On the account of the healing that I received... here you go... My eyes twitched and moved side to side as if looking at a person, or in lecture, staring; my eyes moved around. It wasn't lazy eye but something going on with my nerve circuit and eye muscles. This had been going on for the past year or so and really developed over the past few months of spring and summer quarters. I thought it was the usual lack of sleep, but it wasn't because when I slept, it came back anyway. So over the weekend I went to a talk called, 'I am the Lord your Healer,' given by Brother Bob Canton from Stockton, California. Bro. Bob has a blessed healing ministry and travels all over the world and conducts healing services everywhere, and where God's name is called upon, healings and miracles happen. Well, anyway, we were just praying for one another and he mentioned, 'for those who have glasses take them off, and we'll pray for the eyes.' So we prayed in the Spirit for a while, and healings came: healings of glaucoma, lazy eye, and other eye problems were healed. But for me, while in prayer I felt like a sharp object or knife or laser or something went through my eyes from left to right. It didn't hurt or anything but something was just there. After that, I opened my eyes and I was able to see better without any trouble. My eyes didn't shake anymore, and I just felt the Holy Spirit upon me and I knew in my heart that I was healed from whatever problem I had in my eyes. So in the end… Praise God!

Believe it or not, cause I do… it is your choice… but here's one thing… from any minor to major problems in our lives, we all need healing no matter what, even if we think our lives are good and stable. We need healing within finances, emotions, physical, relationship, family, you name it—we probably need a healing there too. My eye movements seem so minor to other problems people face but in the end, if God allows suffering to happen, He does it for a reason, not because of chastisement or punishment, but for growth within a person's faith and relationship with Him. God's love and mercy is abundant and He gives for our benefit.

John 10:10 says, 'I came so that they might have life and have it more abundantly.' Jesus gave us life to live it properly and carefully but as sinners, we fail miserably, so therefore only by God's grace are we made whole again and transformed to be better people, better children of God.

As the theme for the weekend was 'Be Transformed,' many of the healings and the experiences that people experienced over these past few days were for our transformation for the better. God refines us in ways we don't understand because our human intellect is limited. But in surrendering to God's power through the Holy Spirit, one will be transformed and be strengthened to be an instrument of God. We surrender everything to Him and allow Him to change our lives. In other words, we give it to Him. Let go and let God. We are transformed in mind, heart, and soul, so that by word and deed our lives become the "light"—the Light of God in which our ministry is about— touching others, lifting up one another, so that all of us will be closer to God and be made saints. We all have a long way to go to become saints but the process of fulfilling it is already in progress as we try to live a holy life to be transformed for our own benefit."

—Ryan, Medical Student, UC Irvine Medical School—

"Hi, my name is Tanya Michelle Avendaño, and I was born blind in my left eye. I attended the healing services at St. James Church in McMinnville, Oregon, on October 5, 6, and 7. I was healed by the Lord on Friday, October 5, when Bob Canton was praying for healing over me and I started to see from my left eye after his prayers. I thought I was imagining things, then he asked if there was anyone here who had experienced healing. I raised my hand and praised the Lord for the miracle of giving me my vision in my left eye. This is a miracle that God did for me, as I was completely blind in my left eye. All I can say is that miracles do exist. During the Parish Mass on Sunday morning, October 7, Deacon Raul Rodriguez, during *his homily, asked those who were healed during the Healing Workshop by Bob Canton to please stand. Many stood, including me. I was seated way back by the entrance of the church. From the altar, he asked me to cover my right eye with my hand and to follow his hand movements to test my vision. I was able to follow everything that he did. The world looks different for me now that I can see with both eyes! Praise the Lord! My healing proved that Jesus is truly a loving and healing God."*

—*Tanya Avendano, McMinville, OR*—

Prayer for Healing of Blindness and Other Eye Diseases

Lord Jesus, you are the Healer of our mind, body, soul, and spirit. In you, there is wholeness and healing and restoration. I ask you to saturate my eyes with your most precious blood, the same blood that you shed on the Cross at Calvary. Touch my eyes also through the power of the Holy Spirit the way you touched the blind while you were still walking on this Earth 2,000 years ago. In Jesus' precious Name, I command the spirit of blindness to leave me. I command my pupils, my lenses, the iris and cornea, the retina and sclera, the tissues and the optic nerves, the blood vessels, and cells to function normally, and all parts of my eyes to be at their best conditions in the Name of and by the blood of Jesus. I command the pressure inside the eyes to go down to normal and the drainage canals in the eyes to open up for the fluids to flow through and the macula to be alive and to be rejuvenated and to function normally, and the cataracts to be dissolved completely, in Jesus' Name. Lord, renew also the sharp, central vision of my eyes. I command, in Jesus' Name, my blood sugar, my blood pressure, and my cholesterol to be normal. I speak complete healing into my eyes and I thank you, Jesus, for hearing my prayers. May your Name be glorified through my healing. Praise your Holy Name, Lord Jesus Christ. Amen.

Speaking before the Korean National Catholic Charismatic Convention in Daegu, South Korea. Standing next to Robert is Sr. Gemma Marie, O.S.B., the Korean translator.

Part of the 9,000 who attended a Healing Crusade in Daegu, South Korea.

CHAPTER FIFTEEN

Miraculous Healings of Deafness and Other Ear Diseases

Then Jesus left the vicinity of Tyre and went through Sidon, down to the Sea of Galilee and into the region of the Decapolis. There some people brought to him a man who was deaf and could hardly talk, and they begged Jesus to place his hand on him. After he took him aside, away from the crowd, Jesus put his fingers into the man's ears. Then he spit and touched the man's tongue. He looked up to heaven and with a deep sigh said to him, "Ephphatha!" (which means, "Be opened!"). At this, the man's ears were opened, his tongue was loosened and he began to speak plainly. Jesus commanded them not to tell anyone. But the more he did so, the more they kept talking about it. People were overwhelmed with amazement. "He has done everything well," they said. "He even makes the deaf hear and the mute speak." (Mark 7:31-37)

One of the compelling reasons why Jesus is still healing now is His undying love and compassion for His people. In Matthew 14:14, the Bible says,

Jesus got out of the boat, and when He saw the large crowd, His heart was filled with pity for them, and He healed their sick.

Hebrews 13:5 says,

I will never leave you. I will never forsake you.

Over and over again, I have witnessed deaf people receive their healing. As a matter of fact, I have collections of hearing aids from people who used to wear them. For me, they are indeed reminders of the Lord's awesome power to heal. Beginning on the next page are some of the testimonies about healing of deafness:

"I was not able to hear properly for more than ten years. Then I started using hearing aids for the past two years because I became totally deaf in both ears. At times, I also didn't manage to hear well in spite of using hearing aids.

While attending daily mass, I learned that Bob Canton was coming to Kuching to conduct workshops on Healing and Spiritual Warfare at Blessed Sacrament Center for three successive days. I didn't manage to get a place because they could only accommodate 500 people for the workshop and two weeks before the event, it was totally booked with a long waiting list. But I decided that I must attend the Healing Rally at the church. So I went to the rally on the first night (April 12, 2013). The church was fully packed, standing room only, and many had to stand outside of the church.

When Bob Canton called for those with hearing problems, I quickly got up and somehow found my way to the altar, as there was a long queue. When Bob Canton saw me, he called for me, but I didn't feel nice to jump the queue until one of the organizing committee members led me to him. He asked me what my problem was. I told him I could not hear properly and needed hearing aids for both ears. I was asked to remove them, and Bob prayed over me and commanded the deafness to go in Jesus' Name. At that moment, I really felt the presence of the Lord! Immediately I could hear very much better. Since then I do not need my hearing aids anymore! Praise the Lord for healing me and glory be to God."

—Wivina Poh S.L., Kuching, Sarawak, Malaysia—

"When my granddaughter, Lauren, was six months old, she was diagnosed with moderate hearing loss in both ears. The specialist told my daughter, Agnes, and her husband

*that Lauren would need a hearing aid throughout her life.
They were devastated! Suddenly, the future of their beautiful little girl was cloudy and uncertain. They had lots of
questions on their minds:* Would she learn how to talk?
Would she be able to go to college? Would the other
children be cruel to her? Would I ever hear her call me
Mom? *They prayed for strength but cried every day.*

*I told them to call Bro. Bob Canton in California so
that he could pray over her. They reached him late one
night in California and with their hands pressed on Lauren's ears, who was asleep, Bro. Bob prayed over her on the
telephone. Over the next few weeks, she seemed to respond
to their voices and other noises but they dismissed the signs
as wishful thinking. After a month, they saw their doctor
again for the checkup visit and for Lauren to be fitted
with the hearing aid. They tested her hearing by sending
signals to her ears and monitoring her brain response. Several levels of noise were tested starting with the loudest to
the faintest and she responded to all. She could hear! The
doctor had no explanation. We thank God for answering
our prayers and for this tremendous grace. Lauren is now a
talkative two-and-a-half- year-old toddler who smiles all
the time. She is one of the youngest witnesses to the power
of God."*

—Greg Acedo, Durham, NC—

*"On Friday, February 23, 2007, at Sacred Heart Cath-
olic Church in Bradenton, FL, I received a healing of my*

hearing during a Healing service conducted by you. I had been hearing-impaired for thirty years and wore hearing aids. When you called for those who wear hearing aids to come for prayer, I went up and you prayed over me. I was not there for myself but I was healed. I did not put the hearing aids in again and still don't wear them. I have difficulty at times, but I praise God and I'm claiming the healing and thanking God every day, many times a day. When I have difficulty, I talk to my Healer and praise Him. I want to give testimony to that. My sister was with me and she witnessed it along with some friends, and I'm telling different ones and I'm giving God the glory. I say the healing prayer you gave to everyone every day and continue to praise God and thank Him. I just wanted to give testimony to this. Thank God for your ministry, and I pray for that. I gave a copy of your healing prayer to a friend with bad arthritis in her knees and together we pray for healing. Her name is Gloria. Please pray for her too. Thank you, and God bless you."
—*Theresa E., Bradenton, FL*—

"My husband and I were healed at the Scranton Conference in early August 2005. We both wear hearing aids, but since then have not worn them. We praise the Lord and thank you for laying hands on us for healing. I have heard crickets and the rain on the roof without aid, and it is wonderful. We have given testimony to all we know and find it sad to say that people for the most part do not believe us.

They do not seem to feel that healing like this can occur in the Catholic Church. Isn't that sad? We say the 'Healing and Keeping' prayer daily to reinforce our healing."
—Kenneth and Evelyn H., PA—

"I had been suffering hearing loss and ringing in my left ear since about four years ago. I went to our family doctor here on Lanai and went to a specialist in Honolulu and another doctor on Maui. The last doctor I went to, which was on Maui, told my daughter and me that there is no cure. He did not know whether the hearing would come back and suggested we wait for ten months. Ten months had long passed and it was still the same. With many prayers, sometimes I could hear, but the ringing was bad. Bob Canton came to Lanai, and my daughter called us to go and said do not wait till after the mass. Bob was giving a workshop to our church members. My husband and I went right away. Bob prayed over me and now I can hear clearly in my left ear and the ringing is not as often and intense as before. Thank God."
—Veronica F., Lanai City, HI—

"I attended the entire four days' Healing Workshop and Masses from 14th to 17th February in Singapore.
Day 1 – 14 February (Valentine's Day)
The testimony you gave on how The Good Lord reaches out to you is really out of the extraordinary, and the sharing

of your experiences and cases you dealt with, under His guiding hands, were really enriching. Your talk was broad based, humorous, and captivating. I picked up many lessons as 'I Heard from The Lord.' I shall explain.

I had severe hearing problems with both my ears. My "left ear" was stone-dead since 1992, until you prayed over me. After your prayer over me, I was able to hear some noise, although I couldn't decode the signal nor decipher the actual sound. Doctors told me that the cells behind my eardrums were damaged, and it would continue to be a degenerating effect. It would only get worse and never better. But I did hear very faint and distant sounds. Your assurance that sometimes the Lord treats in installments gave me further hope. I believe, but reverting a seventeen-year-old problem casts doubt.

However, and more important, I actually 'Heard the Lord.' I listened and heard HIM telling me through you that SATAN has a way with us. His evil tactics on obsession, temptation, bondage, infestation, possession, etc., came to me sharply. I went away telling myself that the Lord is passing more important hearing messages. I went home contented that although I hear little physically, I actually hear more spiritually. Whether I will be able to physically hear is almost non-significant, as I have lived with the problem for the past seventeen years. I believe that if GOD wants to heal me, he will do it in His time.

Day 2 – 15 February

I picked up other lessons and continued to see in amazement some of the healings that took place. At the same time I was also doubtful, as I believe some could have reacted as a result of auto-suggestions. However, my own hearing in my left ear was a little better. I did many other actions to try and tell myself that there were no mistakes, that the Good Lord has indeed opened up my ear canal. I was certain that something had happened. When I attended mass that evening, I could almost hear every word during the entire service. This alone is a miracle, as I never was able to sit thru a mass hearing every word spoken by the priests. The Lord was speaking to me!

Day 3 – 16 February

In the Church of the Risen Christ, I took a seat that I often chose, as it provides me the best position to hear the speaker. I normally could pick up about 50 percent of whatever was said. That evening, I was smiling ear-to-ear when you spoke because I could hear you so well. I participated actively that evening and I told my wife that the hearing in my left ear is now perhaps 20 percent as against being stone dead. She was excited too. We rejoiced but did not announce it. My friends and prayer members were concerned and wanted to know whether I could hear since 14 February. I gave them a doubtful thumbs up.

The other miracles I witnessed that evening were so many wheelchair bound fellow Christians standing up to walk, especially a young boy walking around the church, even though you did not pray directly for him. It increased my faith that the Good Lord and the Holy Spirit were indeed present.

Day 4 – 17 February

The crowd this evening swelled to incredible numbers, and everyone was surging forward when the healing began.

My miracle happened when I could hear my wife singing when she stood on my left. I normally hear nothing unless the guy shouts at me, and the hearing also through my right ear was 70 percent working. I continued praying, and her voice became louder and louder. When the healing session for the deaf took place, I went up again. I heard you really good, perhaps 30 to 40 percent. I concluded that the Lord is actually healing me in stages.

Day 5 to Day 14

My hearing improved further. When I listened to music from my cell phone, I was never able to hear with my left ear. Now, I could sing along when I placed the cell phone close to my left ear. What the doctors had declared seventeen years ago, that I would never hear again in my left ear has been remedied by the Good Lord. Although I couldn't hear the stereo effect on music played as yet, I could hear that it was louder. The Lord had now made me able to hear Him physically and spiritually, but in stages. My faith and those of my prayer members, my family members, and by you and all the prayer members from the Roman Catholic Churches from Singapore and Malaysia, in praying over my hearing problems, has been answered.

As Nothing Is Impossible to God, it is only right that the glory of the Good Lord be revealed with a sincere and grateful heart through this testimony."

—David Lim Pheng, Singapore—

"Hi, my name is Theresa Ravago and I used to be completely deaf in my right ear. I am not exactly sure how it
happened and neither do my doctors. It could have been a
birth defect or something that could have caused it at an
early age, but all I know is that I was told not even hearing aids or surgery could help me regain my hearing. The
problem had only come to my attention when I was in the
fourth grade, about nine years ago, my mom whispered
something in my ear while tucking me into bed and I had
not heard her at all. She questioned me asking if I had
and my answer sent her into a panic.

The next day I was in an otolaryngologist's office. They
confirmed my loss of hearing, but their words didn't really
affect me because it's all I've known so I was already accus-
tomed to it. The only problem was, now that I was aware
of my problems, it made me aware of my differences from
others and my personal disability. More times than not, I
had to continuously ask people to repeat themselves do to
the fact that I could not hear them. It was something I
had then become embarrassed about; I've missed out many
things that had been told to me because I feared asking
people to repeat themselves over and over. But one day, I
met Jake Mireles, my boyfriend and Mr. Robert Canton's
nephew, and he had patience with me and my hearing.
And even with such a disability, he cared for me. He introduced me to his family, who welcomed me with open arms.
Once they heard about my hearing loss they offered to pray
over me. The first time was at a healing mass one night

in St. Lukes, by Mr. Robert Canton. The second time, on Mothers day, Jake, Mr. and Mrs. Robert and Chita Canton, Mrs. Alsayegh, Mrs. Mireles, Mrs. Lily Canton, and Father Joe Maghinay of Presentation Parish prayed over me. As they prayed, I closed my eyes. As I felt the love and care that I was surrounded by, I felt Jesus' presence captivate me. And for the first time, I heard and understood what my boyfriend, Jake, whispered in my ear. I began to shed tears of joy, not only because that I could hear again, but also what I had realized at that moment. God has given me these amazing people in my life, people who care for me and even though they haven't known me for very long, they still act like if I was already part of the family. The Lord has been so good to me, and I cannot thank Him enough for all that He has done."

Theresa Ravago—Stockton, CA

"On July 3, 2014, there was a firework at the beginning of the game (I am a student working part time for a triple A baseball team) and after it was over, my boss told me and my grounds crew co-workers to clean up the fireworks debris. As I picked up one of them, I heard a big boom!!. Unexpectedly, a firework cannon went off when it was not supposed to. I thought I was dead because when I tried to get up and stood up, I could see thousands of people on the stadium but I could not hear anything.

I was taken to immediate care right away, and after few testings the doctor told my parents that I had a head concussion and possible a hole in my left eardrum.

The doctor then ordered me to rest and scheduled me to be seen by him again 4 days later for follow up tests. My ear was still very sensitive especially to any sound.

My mom called my uncle Bob right away and asked him to pray over me. I went to my follow up check, this time the doctor referred me to an ear, nose and throat specialist for proper treatment because my ear tests(repeated three times) showed I have a hole in my left eardrum. In the mean time, uncle Bob who was in Southern California at that time to care for his daughter Tricia, prayed for me again over the telephone.

The ENT specialist tested me again, this time, he said it doesn't look like a hole existed anymore. Praise God! I truly believe that our Lord Jesus healed me. Since uncle Bob prayed over me, my hearing came back to normal right away. Everything has been back to normal, no more pain and any sound doesn't hurt my ear. There was also no after effect of the concussion. The Lord Jesus is truly a Healer!!!

Thank you uncle Bob for praying over me and Thank you Lord for healing me!"

— *Jake Canton Mireles, Stockton, CA* —

"I, as a person, am really amazed with what you did in the name of Jesus to many people in Jakarta, Indonesia. This was my first time I saw God's grace in front of my eyes. God really used you mightily in healing many sicknesses like God did to His people. This was the first time for me to see many blind people, many in wheelchairs, many deaf

people and demonized people, and deaf mutes, and people with tumors, receive miraculous healings. Now, I'm just praying for you, Robert, so you can continue your good works and always be blessed by God."

—Gregorios K., Jakarta, Indonesia—

"On June 7, 2008, I was at the Healing Retreat in New Berlin, WI. I was expecting great things and I knew the Lord was working in my life. Bob Canton prayed over me, and I was able to hear. He asked me to walk without my cane, and I did! Since then, I have not used my cane and hearing aids anymore! I broke my back two years ago, and the doctors said they could not do anything anymore. But JESUS, the Divine Physician, can do anything! I was so excited when I went back to my nursing home. I felt like I was bursting out of my skin. I kept sharing what the Lord has done. I give all the power and the honor due to Him!"

—Marjorie T., Menomonee Falls, WI—

"At the healing service, Bob Canton asked those with deafness to come forward, and I did. Then he put his fingers in my ears. I felt a pop, then things sounded louder and clearer. I used to wear hearing aids in both ears, but not anymore after that Healing Service. I give glory and praise to the Lord Jesus Christ for His faithfulness and for hearing our prayers."

—John G., Wisconsin—

"*I went to the Philippines to be with Bob Canton during one of his Healing Crusades. While in Manila, I asked my relatives to attend the first Healing Crusade, which was held in St. Joseph's Church in Forbes Park. One of my relatives in attendance was my seventeen-year old nephew who had been deaf-mute since birth. After the Mass, Bob laid hands on the people who were afflicted with various kinds of sickness and disease. Invoking the precious blood and using the mighty name of Jesus, Bob commanded the deaf and dumb spirit to leave my nephew and implored the Lord to heal him for His glory.*

My nephew was able to hear and to speak some words for the first time in his life! We went home the following day, and news of his healing had spread like wild fire in our town. A few days later, our town had a festival. There were noises all over from firecrackers and from the different marching bands. My nephew, who had never heard these noises before, became hysterical. He put his fingers in his ears and began to scream. Many people had witnessed what happened to my nephew and they believed. In the same Healing Crusade, another nephew of mine who had great difficulty walking as a result of a stroke that he suffered came forward for prayers. As Bob was praying over him, my nephew started to shake. He said he felt heat all over his body, especially his legs. 'In the name of Jesus, I command you to stand up and walk,' Bob said to him. Suddenly, my nephew stood up and walked normally without using his cane. My nephew is now back at work,

completely healed by the Lord Jesus. I also travelled with Bob to Cebu City and Iloilo City. I was awed by the openness of the thousands of people to the Lord during these Crusades. I have witnessed the healings of the lame, the blind, and of course, the deaf-mute. I also heard people giving testimonies that their tumors, cysts, and abnormal growths had disappeared instantly during the Crusades. I had witnessed the glory of Yahweh "burst forth" before us. What I had witnessed and heard has changed my life. I thank Jesus for letting me witness His power and His mighty work. Glory to God!"
　　　　　—*Levy Zindac, Clifton, NJ*—

"My hearing loss due to bone deterioration along with nerve damage to both ears has been a miserable journey for the past thirty-four years. It has gotten to the point of no hope. My ENT doctor, told me that my condition was irreversible and to expect to be totally deaf someday. I am Portuguese and very stubborn. I refuse to accept his diagnosis 'cause I know Jesus, our Healer, can heal anyone at anytime. I have been to many healing services, including your first trip to Hawaii, and nothing happened. Being who I am I continued to pray for healing.

On August 2, 2008, at our HCCRS Conference, I again went up to be prayed over by you and when I returned to my seat, the music was so loud I immediately removed the hearing aid from my right ear. All praises to our Living God! My hearing in both ears is almost normal.

On August 6, 2008, four days later, I had my ears tested by a certified hearing instrument specialist, Mr. Michael S. Baughn/BC-HIS, whom I trust. He was astounded at the results and his exact words were, 'Oh, Wow!' His blue eyes were as big as the size of quarters. Yes, my Jesus in seconds gave me back most of my hearing that I had lost over the years.

Mr. Baughn said that it was impossible for the deteriorated bones to heal. However, I still have nerve damage. This I know, in time, will also be healed. Praise God! He jokingly asked me if he could send some of his patients to our healing services. He also said if anyone wants to verify his test on me, he would more than gladly provide the proof if I would authorize it.

Thank you Jesus! And thank you Bob Canton."

—*Peggy, Honolulu, HI*—

"My husband Nemesio and I accompanied Bob Canton to Singapore to attend the 2nd International Congress of Catholic Charismatic Servant Communities. Bob was one of the invited speakers to address the Congress and he was also invited to conduct a Healing Crusade in Singapore. It was truly a blessing for us to witness the signs and wonders, healings, and miracles in Singapore.

The Healing Crusade, which was held in an indoor stadium, was attended by approximately 10,000 people, including the Archbishop of Singapore. The organizers said that it was one of the biggest, if not the biggest, Healing

Crusades ever held in Singapore. After the Holy sacrifice of the Mass, the Blessed Sacrament was then processed inside the stadium by a priest. Bob exhorted the crowd to believe that the Divine Healer, Jesus Christ, was truly present in their midst, as the Blessed Sacrament was exposed. He led the crowd in praying the "Forgiveness" Prayer and in asking the Lord Jesus for spiritual, physical, and emotional, and most especially, spiritual healings. He then commanded the people in wheelchairs to stand up and walk in the Name of Jesus. Fifteen people walked from the wheelchairs, including a ten-year-old girl who had cerebral palsy. It was the first time for her to walk in her life. Some people gave testimonies that it was the first time for them to walk after ten years of confinement in the wheelchair as a result of paralysis and strokes. What we saw and heard reminded me of the accounts in the Bible when the Lord used Peter to heal the lame person by the Temple called Beautiful. Many people also gave testimonies that their tumors, lumps, and cysts instantly disappeared. There were at least two teenagers who were delivered from oppression of evil spirits. The Lord Jesus truly manifested His presence in that crusade. As matter of fact, many people said that they strongly felt the presence of God. I don't doubt that conversions of many hearts had also taken place.

From Singapore, we also went to the Philippines with Bob, where he conducted a series of Healing Crusades in Manila, Cebu City, and Iloilo City. Fr. Leonardo Polinar, a well known priest from the Philippines, also accompanied Bob to these crusades. In that Healing Crusade in

Manila, a seventeen-year-old boy who was born deaf-mute was able to hear and speak for the first time in his life. I saw a large tumor in a woman's neck become indistinguishable and an elderly lady who was able to move her once frozen arm. I also saw people walk from their wheelchairs and throw away their canes and walkers during the Healing Crusade.

In Cebu City, similar healings took place, including that of a twenty-two-year-old woman who had been blind in both eyes since birth. More miracles and healings happened in a gymnasium in Iloilo City. Bob exhorted the people to renounce the superstitious beliefs and to surrender their lucky charms and amulets. Many people did as Bob had asked them to do by putting their amulets and lucky charms into a big garbage can, which Bob had placed on the side of the stage. Afterwards, numerous healings took place; the lame were able to walk, the blind had their eyesight restored, and the deaf were able to hear. As these healings and miracles were taking place, I heard people asking the Lord for forgiveness of their sins. Bob had emphasized the fact that sin, unforgiveness, hatred, and resentment are the blockages to healing.

I, myself, was the recipient of God's healing grace. A few years ago, I was diagnosed as having a gall stone. However, I had refused to undergo surgery. A few months ago, I had another attack of symptoms similar to the previous ones. I started attending the prayer meetings and healing services at St. Luke's Parish and I always asked for prayers for healing. Not long afterwards, I went to see my doctor, who scheduled me for more tests, including an ultrasound. The doctor was astounded by the test results. My gall stone had disappeared without a trace. I can truly say that Jesus Christ is my Savior and my Healer. My husband and I are thankful to Bob Canton and to the Children of God Prayer Community of St. Luke's for ministering to us in the Name of Jesus. Our lives have never been the same again. Praise the Lord now and forever!"

—Norma Lebrilla, Sacramento, CA—

Prayer for Healing of Deafness and Other Ear Diseases

"Thank you, Lord, for creating me out of love. I believe that you can also recreate me. I ask you now to touch my ears by the power of the Holy Spirit to restore my hearing.

Lord, heal the cause or causes of deafness such as infections or structural problems, or eardrum perforation, nerve damage, or narrowing of the ear canal or physical trauma that I might have sustained that caused the hearing loss, or any other causes that are not known to me. My Jesus, renew and rejuvenate and speak life to all the parts of my ears; the cochlea, auditory nerves, semicircular canal, pinna, ear canal, eardrum, hammer, anvil, stirrup, eustachian tube.

In Jesus' Name, I take authority over the spirit of deafness and I command it to leave me right now, and I command my ears to open up and the ringing in my ears to stop and be healed completely. I apply by faith, the most precious blood and the healing touch of Jesus into all the parts of my ears. Thank you Jesus, the Master Healer, for what you are doing right now and what you are going to do so that I can hear normally.

May you be glorified through my healing. I ask all of these in Jesus' precious Name, Amen."

CHAPTER SIXTEEN

Miraculous Healings of Paralysis and Other Walking Disabilities

A few days later, when Jesus again entered Capernaum, the people heard that He had come home. They gathered in such large numbers that there was no room left, not even outside the door, and He preached the word to them. Some men came, bringing to Him a paralyzed man, carried by four of them. Since they could not get him to Jesus because of the crowd, they made an opening in the roof above Jesus by digging through it and then lowered the mat the man was lying on. When Jesus saw their faith, He said to the paralyzed man, "Son, your sins are forgiven."

Now some teachers of the law were sitting there, thinking to themselves, "Why does this fellow talk like that? He's blaspheming! Who can forgive sins but God alone?"

Immediately Jesus knew in His spirit that this was what they were thinking in their hearts, and He said to them, "Why are you thinking these things? Which is easier: to say to this paralyzed man, 'Your sins are forgiven,' or to say, 'Get up, take your mat and walk'? But I want you to know that the Son of Man has authority on earth to forgive sins." So He said to the man, "I tell you, get up, take your mat and go home." He got up, took his mat and walked out in full view of them all. This amazed everyone, and they praised God, saying, "We have never seen anything like this!" (Mark 2:1-12)

In Acts 3:1-10, we read,

One day Peter and John were going up to the temple at the time of prayer—at three in the afternoon. Now a man who was lame from birth was being carried to the temple gate called Beautiful, where he was put every day to beg from those going into the temple courts. When he saw Peter and John about to enter, he asked them for money. Peter looked straight at him, as did John. Then Peter said, "Look at us!" So the man gave them his attention, expecting to get something from them.

Then Peter said, "Silver or gold I do not have, but what I do have I give you. In the name of Jesus Christ of Nazareth, walk." Taking him by the right hand, he helped him up, and instantly the man's feet and ankles became strong. He jumped to his feet and began to walk. Then he went with them into the temple courts, walking and jumping, and praising God. When all the people saw him walking and praising God, they recognized him as the same man who used to sit begging at the temple gate called Beautiful, and they were filled with wonder and amazement at what had happened to him.

It is truly a faith-building experience to see the lame able to walk. "For God, nothing is impossible at all." It is really a very uplifting experience when people come to me and give me their cane or walker or foot braces or orthopedic shoes, because they were able to walk normally after they received prayers for healing. As a result, I have collections of canes, walkers, and foot braces. One time, a lady from Piscataway, New Jersey, offered to give me her wheelchair because she was able to walk after being confined in that wheelchair for five years. I told her, however, that it would be difficult for me to check it in at the airport for my flight back to California. I advised her to donate the wheelchair to a charitable organization.

Here are some of the testimonies about healing of paralysis and other walking disabilities by the Divine Healer.

"I just attended a wonderful Healing Rally by Robert Canton over the last two nights at the Church of the Risen Christ in Singapore. This was the first time I had attended something to do with healing at a church. The energy, when we walked in, was really strong, and there was an air of expectancy all around.

The first day we were a little late, but still the ushers greeted us happily, and we managed to get a pretty good seat near the band. They had started off with some praise and worship songs, and the presence of the Holy Spirit was definitely there.

So, after the songs Bob appeared on stage and talked a bit about himself, as an introduction and got some people who had experienced healings to give testimonies. It sounds amazing, but what we would see later on would be more amazing. Bob emphasized, though, that he is not the healer, that the healings came from God, and he is just there to pray for the sick.

The healings started, and many miracles happened. Many people had come in wheelchairs, and amazingly all of them got out of them, even one who was paralyzed. She was still having problems with her speech, but she got out of her chair. Most of them walked quite a distance; amazing, considering they had not gotten out of their wheelchairs for years. And there was this little boy. I think he was the inspiration for the day. He was so happy to be out of his wheelchair without any help, that he walked round and round the church and praised the Lord. That was the first time for him to get out of the wheelchair as he had been paralyzed since birth.

The second day he brought his mom, and more miracles happened, but what was close to my heart for me, was that he and his mom went up and experienced the healing themselves. I guess with this sort of thing, you truly feel touched when someone close, or yourself, actually experiences it. In fact, I think many people went back and told others, because on the second day we were early, but it was already packed and we almost couldn't find a seat.

I thank God for Bob Canton, for coming to Singapore to give this Healing Rally. God is awesome; He truly is."

—*Joan P., Singapore*—

"Yesterday, I went to a healing conference together with my mom and older sister in Silay City. Since it was scheduled to start around 9:30 A.M., we had to wake up early at 4:00 A.M. and get ready for the long trip, since it would take around two hours via bus from Escalante. By the time we reached Silay, we stopped at the El Real bakeshop to eat some snacks, then my mom entrusted someone

owning a cell phone load business to carry her luggage and keep it in her store for the time being, to avoid hassle.

By the time we reached the venue, there were many in wheelchairs and those who were either born or just afflicted deaf-mute. As a start, we first had some form of energizer in the form of dances, then afterward a fifteen-minute break, then the morning Mass.

After another energizer, we finally listened to the words of Bro. Bob Canton, the guest speaker. He inspired us with words of wisdom, that we must forgive, humble ourselves, and confess. However, the most touching event was during his healing session. It was indeed a miracle to behold. Can you imagine those who were crippled in wheelchairs being able to walk, or even deaf-mute people being able to hear and speak, with just powerful words and a healing touch? Even I experienced that, too, for when I felt God's healing power, I suddenly fell on the floor for a few seconds, but in the end I was able to stand straight.

Now that I've experienced such a miracle, I now believe that I must not lose hope, for miracles only happen once we have faith in God."

— *Mary Anne T., Escalante, Negros Oriental, Philippines*—

"Thank you so much dear Brother Bob for praying over my mom two weeks ago in Astoria, N.Y. You remember the lady in the wheelchair who was able to walk and then to dance with you and asked you to sit down on the wheelchair? She was pushing the wheelchair with you in it

around inside the church? Well she looks and feels ten years younger, and everyone is amazed by the improvement! She is now doing things that she has not been able to do in the last ten years or so! Hope your ministry continues to grow through the years, and we continue to pray for you and yours, and everyone who comes to you for healing. Best of luck and blessings on all your future endeavors and may we all continue to be protected by Mother Mary's maternal care. Hope to see you once again here in Astoria in the very near future. Many people are waiting for your return. Happy Thanksgiving!"
—Gina C., Astoria, NY—

"My name is Sara, and I want to share a story with you. About two-and-a-half years ago we received a call from our niece who lives in Puebla, Mexico, and we live in El Paso, TX. She called to inform us that our other niece, Julisa, was at the hospital and her condition was very critical. At this time, I want to give you a bit of background of our family. My nephew in Mexico was living a promiscuous life, and his wife was not aware of his affairs with other women. He became ill, and no one knew why or how he died. He was in his mid twenties. At the time of his death, his wife was pregnant, and she had a baby named Julisa. After her birth, Julisa's mother became ill and had the same symptoms her husband had. The doctors discovered she had AIDS. Julisa's mother passed away a few months after her birth. Julisa was born with HIV, both of her parents

had passed, and my sister became mother and father to her three grandkids. Julisa has always had health problems, but never to the point to be hospitalized. The primary doctor told my sister to make arrangements because Julisa was not going to make it through the weekend. They were giving her a few days of life, and we could not believe what was happening, as she was only nine years old at the time and full of life. She was telling everyone she did not want to die, She wanted a new dress and shoes from the US for Christmas. Christmas was a month away, and everyone thought she was going to pass in a few days; she was in and out.

My Compadres (Godparents to my children) Pablo and Irma, told us in the past that we should go to a conference, that a man by the name of Bob Canton was going to be coming and through him God has done a lot of miracles. When they spoke about this, we smiled and we said sure, ah ha. Needless to say, we did not attend any of the conferences when he came down.

We remember about Bob when we were so desperate that we just did not have any hope left. We went to see Irma about this situation, and we talked about it for a while and as soon as I stopped talking, she told me that she was going to pray for Julisa's health. We told her Julisa could not travel to California where Bob lived. She laughed and said she would send an e-mail to Bob Canton and to their prayer circle to pray for Julisa. She said, have faith, for with God there is no distance, and Julisa does not have to travel to CA. At that time we were trying to collect money to help my sister with funeral expenses, which was another reason we went to see them, and they said they would be glad to help but that she is not going to go die. They said God has plans for Julisa; you will see. I had to believe what I was told because they are wonderful people that pray when we are in need. A couple of days later, we received another call from Mexico, and my heart fell to the floor. I asked when did Julisa pass? They told me it was a miracle that Julisa was out of the hospital and, surprisingly, all of her symptoms were gone. The doctors do not understand what happened, but we know that God saved her, and since that moment Julisa has been wonderfully doing great every day. That is why I want to thank God for saving her, and thank Bob Canton and his ministry for the prayers. We cannot stop thanking God for the miracle. Julisa is almost twelve, and this coming November will be three years since the miracle. We traveled to Mexico this March, and Julisa is a normal girl and has gone back to school and is full of life.

We were blessed to have had the opportunity to meet Bob Canton in El Paso about a year ago. This time we went to see him in person—not for prayer, but to thank him and God. While I do not speak English, I did hear his talk through a translator that was provided. In any language, a miracle is a miracle. When Bob prayed over a young lady, she received her hearing, as she was born deaf. I saw a man that could hardly walk dance up and down the aisles, and he no longer uses a cane and he gave the cane to Bob. There were so, so many miracles that night;

I felt like God was inside of me even if Bob did not pray over me.

My daughter is writing this letter for me. I was asked to write it a long time ago, but I do not write in English.

Once again, thank you Bob for your prayers not only for Julisa, but also for my entire family. We now believe, and our faith has grown. We know God is using Bob to change peoples' lives all over the world. He has touched people he has never even met, because my family in Mexico and in the United States all know of Bob."

—*Sara, Puebla, Mexico, and El Paso, TX*—

"Praise the Lord, now and forever! God is good, all the time!

I am writing this e-mail from Sharjah, UAE, with a firm hope you will respond to me. Yesterday I attended your healing session and was mesmerized to see the healings that took place, especially people with hearing aids could later hear without the aids, and persons with crutches and in wheelchairs could walk. I had not experienced any such healing sessions before. Thank you Brother Canton.

Brother Canton, I had an experience during the healing session, which I cannot forget. When you laid hands on me, I went down on the floor. I saw a bright light above me and I felt the presence of God all over me. I felt overwhelmed. The sense of God's presence remained with me for a few more days. I felt as if God had been telling me that He loves me. I could never forget that experience, ever. Is it normal to feel this way? Thank you Jesus! Praise you Jesus!

As promised, be assured of my daily prayers for you, your family, and your ministry. Brother Canton, I look forward to your coming again next year. Our prayer group leaders told us that they are going to do their best to get you back to Dubai again. Many thanks."

—Gladys, Alfridi, and Angell, Dubai, UAE—

"Hi! I am Jocelyn and I was an attendee of the Kerygma Conference that was held last November 28-29 at the Araneta Coliseum in Cubao Quezon City, Philippines, which was attended by around 10,000 people. I was really moved by the healings we witnessed such as the lame walking, the blind seeing, the deaf hearing again, and other wonderful healings. Praise God for that. My parents lined up for healing and they were really healed! My parents have been complaining of difficulty walking because of arthritis, and after the healing session they were able to walk a long distance without pain. They have been walking pain-free since then.

Two days ago, I had a migraine and I followed the prayer you taught us. I prayed 'By the power of the most precious blood of Jesus Christ, poured over me, from the top of my head to the soles of my feet, my headache will be gone, in the name of my Savior, Jesus Christ, I will be healed!' I repeatedly said that and meditated on it. Lo and behold, my headache was gone in minutes, without me having to take any medication. I really thank God for that. Praise God for His miracles.

I am writing this to you to let you know that I am a living testament to God's miracles and healing. I pray that He will continue to use you as His instrument for His healing. I feel truly blessed knowing you. In my own simple way, I will continue to share my experiences to people I know to tell them that God's healing is always present, and it only takes a simple faith to call upon Him in the name of Jesus. God bless you!"

—Jocelyn L., Quezon City, Philippines—

"In 2005, I was diagnosed with Spinal Stenosis—Lumbar Spinal Stenosis classification, and external resources Lumbar vertebra showing central stenosis and lateral recess stenosis. Lumbar Spinal Stenosis (LSS) is a medical condition in which the spinal canal narrows and compresses the spinal cord and nerves at the level of the lumbar vertebra. This is usually due to the common occurrence of spinal degeneration that occurs with aging. It can also sometimes be caused by spinal disc herniation, osteoporosis, or a tumor. In the cervical (neck) and lumbar (low back) region it can be a congenital condition to varying degrees. Spinal stenosis may affect the cervical or thoracic region, in which case it is known as cervical spinal stenosis or thoracic spinal stenosis. In some cases, it may be present in

all three places in the same patient. Lumbar spinal stenosis results in low back pain as well as pain or abnormal sensations in the legs, thighs, feet or buttocks, or loss of bladder and bowel control.

My doctors at Kaiser Medical Center in Los Angeles recommended a battery of medications, which left me feeling like a zombie. I could not do my job or function normally and spent the day in bed sleeping up to 18 hours a day. I would wake up to take more pills for the pain and go back to sleep. I was assigned Neurontin and OxyCodone (with OxyContin), horribly addicitve and damaging drugs. I prayed not to become dependent on them and took these pills until 2006 as per doctor's orders and ended up in an almost vegetative state. I was depressed and I was not living.

Someone from our parish church recommended that I attend the SCRC 2006 convention in Anaheim, and so I packed up my walker and medications and attended the convention. I wandered from workshop to workshop and attended one with Bob Canton. During the healing session and prayer you asked if anyone was suffering from a back problem, and I went up with my walker. I walked up with my walker to receive a blessing for my painful back problems and sat down.

About three to four weeks later, I felt stronger and wanted to lead a more active/productive life. I got out of bed and went to Mass to thank God for my new strength. I hated the medications and stopped taking them, wrapped them up in a big plastic bag, and got rid of them. I am much stronger now and walk five or more miles a day, which is way beyond my expectations.

I have had X-rays following my bout with spinal problems, and the doctors/technicians say that there is evidence of surgery and healing on my back. I tell them that I have never ever had back surgery. This leaves them very puzzled. They could not fully explain what happened to me. I still have a little bit of pain but I manage it with over-the-counter acetaminophen and Vitamin B tablets.

I am grateful to God for your healing hands and prayers. Thanks be to God for His mercy in healing me and for your ministry." In Cristo Rey,

—Michael Roy, Altadena, CA—

"My name is Stephen Berinoe. I am forty-seven years old and I work in the medical field. Sometime before the Healing Crusade, I had been diagnosed with Prolapsed Intervertebral Disc, which resulted in so much pain that I could not walk. I had suffered this before in 2003 (first episode) then I had a relapse on April 4, 2008. I had to attend the Healing Crusade in a wheel chair. I had been bedridden for three weeks.

On May 8, 2008, at about 8.30 P.M. on the first night of the Healing Rally, at the start of the healing session, Bob called for those in wheelchairs to come forward for prayer. My family members wheeled me forward, and Brother Bob prayed over me and then he asked me to walk.

I found I not only could walk but also after a little while, I could eventually run!

I feel very much better, and I am not using the wheelchair anymore. Glory to God!"
—Stephen Berinoe-Sarawak, Kuching, Malaysia—

"On December 2, our parish experienced wonderful and exceptional blessings from the Lord. Brother Bob Canton and his wife Chita from Stockton, California, along with Deacon Leo and his wife Fe Lacbain of Oxnard, California, and Aida Javier of Holy Family Church, Honolulu, came to Lanai to lead a healing service. Fr. Rex, assisted by Deacon Leo, opened the healing service with the celebration of the Holy Mass at 5:00 P.M., after which Bro. Bob gave a very informative presentation about the "Power of the Eucharist To Heal." He mentioned that during the Consecration when the priest invokes the Holy Spirit to turn the bread and wine into the Body and Blood of Christ, a process called "transubstantiation" takes place. In other words, the substance of the bread and the wine will be transformed into the Body and Blood of Jesus Christ. Wow! We are really blessed, because every time we take part wholeheartedly in the Mass, a miracle always takes place. We Catholics believe that a miracle is always happening in our Roman Catholic Churches when Mass is celebrated, and we are joined with God the Father and with Jesus Christ and with his angels and saints gathered around the altar. We have to believe that Jesus Christ is truly present in the Eucharist. Therefore, the Eucharist is the greatest source of healing, because Jesus Christ, our Healer, is truly present in the Eucharist.

*At the healing service after the Mass, a testimony of Jesus'
healing was truly seen in our church when Bro. Bob prayed
over Mrs. Addie Dinong in Jesus' Name! After she was prayed
over, and with the Grace from our Lord, Addie could walk
normally and has not used the wheelchair ever since. During
the healing service, she walked from the wheelchair and she
even asked Bro. Bob to sit in the wheelchair and she pushed it
from the doors of our church down to the altar.*

*We thank and praise You, Jesus, for healing Mrs. Dinong!
And we thank You, Lord, for all the other healings that you
have done in our Parish and community during this healing service."*

—Nora Etrata, Lanai, HI—

*"In Denmark the secularized clouds seem to overshadow
the life-giving and shining light of the Holy Spirit. Despite
the hard efforts from many good, devoted Catholics, we
sometimes get the impression that the Holy Spirit has "left
the building." Whether we have forgotten or unconsciously
neglected the Holy Spirit, I cannot tell, but it is very natural
that Danish Catholics consider the nine charismatic gifts of
the Holy Spirit as just being a "sweet fairy tale" involving
elements not practiced or outdated in these modern times.
But no, this is not the truth. The Holy Spirit is indeed alive
more than ever. Why, you may ask? Look around you. The
Holy Spirit is needed perhaps more than ever.*

*Seeing the power of the Holy Spirit for the first time
in my life, the power of it is unbelievable. I had the great*

privilege and was given the great blessing of following the preacher, Robert Canton, and his wife Chita when they were in Denmark to show and give testimony of the healing power of Jesus. From the thirteenth to the fifteenth of April, Bob Canton held a retreat and led healing services in Saint Anne's Church in Copenhagen. What an incredible sight during the healing service! You could practically see people's jaws hitting the floor. The healings were spectacular. On the first day several elderly persons with walking disabilities (some walking with canes and crutches), after they had been prayed over, were literally jogging in the center aisle of the church—jogging! Deaf could hear again; no need for any hearing devices. People with different sorts of problems and pains in their necks, shoulders, or backs were healed. A woman's sight improved. A man testified that his psoriasis was improving. People suffering from depression and anxiety attacks were healed. A woman with a hole in her heart was healed and gave testimony. Women who had abortions were healed from their guilty feelings. Relationships were being restored...I could go on.... Only Jesus knows the exact number of the healings that took place these days in Copenhagen.

Listen to the final departing words of Our Savior before He was taken up to Heaven (Mark 16:17-19): 'And these signs shall accompany them that believe: In my name shall they cast out demons; they shall speak with new tongues; they shall take up serpents, and if they drink any deadly thing, it shall in no wise hurt them; they shall lay hands on the sick, and they shall recover.' Thank You, Jesus. Thank you.

The next stop was Saint Knud Lavard's Church in Lyngby, on the seventeenth of April. Bob gave a lesson in "gifts of the Holy Spirit," followed by Mass and a healing service. Again, eyes looked like they were about to pop out, meaning, it is not a normal sight for us Danes to see God working healing miracles in front of our very own eyes: A woman could walk again, deaf could hear again, and people suffering from arthritis, diabetes, or problems in the gastrointestinal regions were healed. What impressed me the most that day was Bob telling who and in what way Jesus was healing them. When the priest was blessing people with the monstrance in the form of a cross, Bob mentioned anonymously different people and said aloud their story. Stories for which there is no chance he could have known if they weren't from the Holy Spirit. For example, Bob mentioned my friend's mother who had a tendency to develop kidney stones. Bob mentioned exactly how many times she had been hospitalized, and that Jesus was healing her. Another example: a good friend of mine came up to Bob to get prayed over. Bob asked him whether there was a woman in his family who had cancer. My friend told him that his aunt had cancer, and Bob prayed over him and over his aunt through my friend. Another dear friend of mine had been going through a really tough time. Traumatic experiences from her childhood made her depressed. She was hospitalized and not so long ago she tried to end it all. When the priest was blessing the parishioners with the monstrance, Bob retold her story and let her know that Jesus was healing her from her depression and her guilty feeling. Again, these stories are only a fraction of the healings that took place; healings I and the other parishioners saw and encountered that day. Every single person that came to this healing service must have had his or her own untold healing story only seen by God. And every single person left the healing service healed with whatever needed to be healed. Praise the Lord, forever and forever!

The nineteenth to twenty-second of April, Bob continued his lecture and healing service, praying over people with his wife, Chita, in Saint Nikolaj's Church in Esbjerg. I am only able to mention a fraction of what I saw, but again we witnessed people leaving their wheelchairs, deaf hearing again, people aching from different skeletal problems and joint pains healed. These people came the following day to share their testimonies to the other parishioners. People with heart problems, hypertension, angina, thyroid problems, irritable bowel syndrome, ulcer, problems with the tearglands, etc., were also healed. It was a very beautiful sight. To see the joy, the facial expressions of people who came the next days to share their testimonies; it was absolutely beautiful. To quote the parish priest: 'My parish is never going to be the same again.'

What about me, writing this little testimony? Well, when people speak of healing, they often automatically refer to the physical part of the body. People often forget that the most important healing is to be found in the soul, in the heart, in your relationship with God. What matters if you have a healthy body but your spirit is struggling to survive in a way you are not able to express but only God knows, sees, and understands? After Bob and Chita prayed over me, the inner spiritual knot and the depressive state of mind I had been carrying around were replaced with profound peace. I haven't lost any weight, but it feels like my spirit lost 200 kilos. Whatever happens in a fighting spirit, no words will ever be able to express it. No psychologist, psychiatrist, spiritual director, or priest is able to completely understand the depth of a soul, nor, for that matter, heal it. Only Jesus knows all that needs healing. And only Jesus knows how to completely heal that soul. From the bottom of my heart, thank You, Jesus. Thank You so much for giving me exactly what I needed! And as if this inner healing wasn't enough, I haven't had any migraine attacks since Bob and Chita prayed over me.

What is left to say, Jesus knows all that needs healing. I would like to emphasize that Jesus is the only Healer. The power is being given to faithful servants such as Brother Bob. Jesus wants to transform us for the glory of our Heavenly Father. These miracles that happened in Denmark when Bob prayed over people will change us into more devoted spiritual beings, for thanks to them, we will grow in closer union with God. God only wants us to be little children, asking in love, lifting our hearts to Him in prayer. We should pray. Pray without ceasing, pray for healing. We must lift up our voices in prayer and ask with humble and reverent hearts. GOD will bless us beyond imagination and use us as witnesses in days to come. The only thing required is that we have an open heart and pray for whatever is needed, whether it be of any physical, emotional, spiritual, or psychological character. How God chooses to heal you is solely deter-mined by our Heavenly Father. Perhaps God will send you His faithful servant, Brother Bob.

I strongly encourage everyone to go to a healing ser-vice with Bob Canton. Thank you, Bob, for saying yes to be a powerful instrument of God's love. In times like these God needs hearts open to His grace and mercy with which to work miracles in the lives of many. You are one of those who responded with an open heart. Thank you for ministering and being Jesus' hands, eyes, lips, and healing touch in this broken world some call home."

—Linda Nielsen, Copenhagen, Denmark—

"I attended the Life In the Spirit Seminar this week-end conducted by Bob Canton from California. I was sit-ting in my wheelchair with tight hands and feet, which I frequently suffer from due to Multiple Sclerosis, and as Brother Bob prayed over me and laid his hands on me, I truly felt both my hands and my feet freed of all tight-ness. I've had Relapsing Remitting Multiple Sclerosis for eighteen years now and can't remember ever feeling them free of that tightness. I attribute this, first of all, to Jesus, my Healer, and also to Robert Canton's prayers, his rela-tionship to the Lord and manner of his ministering and teaching, and the way he touches all of those present at his renewals of the Holy Spirit, to have caused this miracle. After sharing this testimony with so many fellow Catholics

there, the sense of unity and goodness was so very present to me and all those around me."
—*Maruschka Villa, Cape Corral, FL*—

"Several years ago, I severely fractured my left ankle and joint (no pins were put in). A few months later, both disintegrated. When the joint broke up, it cut my leg bone in half and they wound up in my foot. Amputation could have been a possibility, but with a plastic brace and a walker, I was able to get around with much difficulty. My leg and foot were stiff and numb. My doctor thought that it was remarkable that I could walk at all.

Bob Canton came to the Holy Redeemer Church in Kissimee, FL, to conduct a workshop on healing and a Healing Service. He prayed over me, and there was much improvement in my condition. Feelings and sensations came back, I could wiggle my toes more easily, the heel and leg bones were looser, and I was able to move with a more comfortable motion. There has been much improvement and ever since then, I have been able to walk without my walker. Everyone notices how well I'm doing. Even my doctor noticed. He said to thank Bob Canton for the prayers. He said that it was incredible that I am walking. He stated that anyone reading my X-rays and X-ray reports would conclude that I could not walk. My split leg bone and another bone have taken over and act like a joint now. Logic and medical findings indicate that I cannot walk, but we know that anything is possible with God. With

great joy, praise and thanksgiving to God, I submit this letter of testimony for His glory."
—Shirley Ratzenberger, Kissimee, FL—
P.S. My doctor said he would sign, too.
(Sgd.) Michael E. Smith, M.D., Kissimee, FL

"Bob Canton invited my husband, Al, and I to attend a meeting of the Alliance of Filipino Catholic Charismatic Prayer Communities, held in Piscataway, New Jersey, on Friday and Saturday, March 7 to 8, 2007. While packing our luggage for the trip, I twisted and sprained my right ankle, and it was hurting during the trip. I tried to walk the long distance from the terminal to the monorail in Newark's International Airport, but found it impossible, so part of the way we asked to be transported by one of those airport mini-cars. While descending to the ground floor by the escalator, a piece of runaway luggage came crashing down the escalator steps, knocked the carry-on bag I was holding out of my hand, and in the ensuing commotion I twisted my injured ankle some more. We missed the core group meeting in the evening because I had to lie down and elevate my right foot. I placed it on an ice pack that Al hurriedly devised from hotel ice cubes and a plastic laundry bag. Al gave me Lodine and warned me about a slow healing process. We were planning to call the airline for wheelchair service and Al was also considering giving me a crutch to use. During the Saturday morning meeting, Bob Canton noticed that I was limping and in

pain. He took me aside and offered to pray over me. I was very grateful for his taking the time from his morning talks to pray over me and ask for healing. That was around 9:00 A.M. By 11:00 A.M., I had a prompting to go to the ladies' room to take off the elastic bandage that I had on my ankle. I obeyed the prompting. When I took the bandage off, the pain was gone and the swelling had also subsided. I went back to my seat, at first in disbelief, but later during the lunch break, when I joined the food line, I truly realized that I was pain-free and in comfort. Praise the Lord. I walked normally the rest of the day. We visited my sister in Toms River both Saturday night and Sunday, and thoroughly enjoyed our reunion completely free of pain and walking normally. Our plane trip back home was much more enjoyable than our trip going to New Jersey. Our prayer group meets on Friday evenings and I shared this healing experience with my friends, which has been a sign of God's love and healing power, and to thank Bob Canton for his ministry of healing."

—*Terri Albarracin, Columbus, OH*—

"The miracle that happened to our father Chinh Ha was spectacular! From being a wheelchair bound person, he stood up, walked around the hall, and finally pushed the wheelchair with you sitting on it! The miracle was from God, but God made the miracle through you. My father had been confined in a wheelchair for eight and a half years. My family decided to come and attend the healing service, which you conducted during the Northern California Catholic Charismatic Conference in Santa Clara, when this miracle happened.

Our family would like to send you deep thanks for what you have done for us. The entire family and our friends are rejoicing right now. We ask God to continue to bless you so that you can transfer His blessings to people. If you happen to have certain pictures or video clips about the event, please share them with us. Thank you very much."

—*Vince Nguyen, San Jose, CA*—

"Thank you so much for coming as our honored international preacher and healer in the 24th AIRCKABS Regional Charismatic Conference in San Carlos City, Negros Occidental, Philippines, on April 24 to 26, 2009.

Great praise and thanksgiving be given to God for the healing miracles He has done to His people through your ministry in San Carlos City on April 25.

See how good God is, when more than ten people confined to wheelchairs were healed and then climbing back and forth on the stage, walking and running. Many people who were blind received sight, including a child who was born blind. Many deaf could then hear and the deaf-mute children (eight to twelve years old) could speak and hear. Two women in maroon dresses and two men in blue shirts who all tried to commit suicide had been healed and delivered from spirit of suicide and from self-condemnation. Many people testified healings and the disappearance of their tumors and cysts and other diseases.

The healings in San Carlos City were repeated when we went for a Healing Crusade in Dumaguete City. On the final day, as an act of thanksgiving at our dinner that night, we prayed over the host who had been deaf for many years. Our host was then instantly able to hear.

Again, in Iloilo City on April 28, all those that were in wheelchairs were able to walk and run. All those who were blind were able to see again, and the deaf could hear. As always the deaf-mute people had dramatic healings.

Our last day of the healing conference, on April 29 in Silay City (Bacolod), created a new dimension. It was so amazing when healings happened to many deaf-mute children, ages two to four years old, that tears fell from my eyes. You only had to lay your hands quickly and yet instant healings of the deaf-mute children happened. How great is our God. His love and mercy is without end. We will always pray for you and your family, Brother Bob.

May God empower you with His gifts more intensely and strongly for the greater glory of His name. Brother Bob, Jesus is alive in your ministry.

Thank you, and we wish that you will come back to Negros, as you have promised, in the near future."

—*Rev. Fr. Nick Domocol, Negros Oriental, Philippines*—

"My friend, Anita Alcantara, invited me to attend a Healing and Miracle Service that was conducted by Bob Canton at St. Catherine of Sienna Church in Manhattan,

New York. I attended the Healing and Miracle Service because my left foot was fractured and I couldn't walk. I had a plaster cast around my foot and I was in a wheel-chair. I was in excruciating pain. During the service, Bob said he had a prompting from the Holy Spirit to pray over me. Then he laid hands on me and prayed to the Lord to make my fractured bones fuse together and the swelling and the pain to disappear completely in Jesus' Name. He also asked the Lord Jesus in faith to lay His healing hands on my fractured foot. Then a few minutes later, Bob com-manded me to stand up and walk in Jesus' Name. When I stood up, I found out that the pain had disappeared. I walked around inside the church with no pain or diffi-culty at all. In fact, I could have run around inside the church. I kept on saying, 'Thank you Jesus, thank you Jesus, I praise you Jesus, I praise you Jesus.' I could not hold back my tears of joy!

The following day I reported back to work wearing my high heeled shoes to the amazement of my fellow employees. This one miracle in my life has truly changed me. Jesus indeed is my Healer!"

—*Anita B. Brion, Brooklyn, NY*—

Prayer for Healing of Paralysis and Other Walking Disabilities

Lord Jesus, I trust in your love for me. I believe, that you can cause me to walk again for your glory and honor. Do unto me as you did to the lame in Capernaum and the paralytic sitting by the pool of Bethesda for you are the God of the impossible and you are not limited by space, or time, or distance. In Jesus' Name, I command the spirit of paralysis and all the possible causes of paralysis such strokes, brain aneurysm, head and spinal cord injuries, multiple sclerosis and other causes, known or unknown, to be completely healed and I speak restoration and strength into my entire body. I apply by faith, the powerful and living blood of Jesus into all parts of my brain; the cerebellum, the lobes, the limbic system, the brain stem so that my brain will be in its best condition ever. Lord Jesus, touch, enliven and rejuvenate my motor system, the primary motor cortex, nerves, the nerve cells, motor neurons, bones, joints, ligaments, and muscles and all parts of my body by the power of the Holy Spirit so that I will be able to walk. In Jesus name, I command all physical aches and pains and any swelling in my body to disappear completely. Lord Jesus, empower my body for me to be able to walk in your Name. Thank you Lord Jesus, the Divine Physician, for hearing my prayers. May your Name be glorified through my healing. Amen.

Speaking on, "How To Be A Miracle Worker for the Glory of God" during the Hispanic Catholic Charismatic Conference in Anaheim Convention Center, Anaheim, CA. Standing next to Robert is Vicky, the Spanish translator.

Part of the attendees during the Hispanic Catholic Charismatic Convention in the Anaheim Convention Center, Anaheim, CA.

CHAPTER SEVENTEEN

Miraculous Healings of Infertility and Barrenness

In Luke 1:5-24, we read,

In the days of Herod, King of Judea, there was a priest named Zechariah of the priestly division of Abijah; his wife was from the daughters of Aaron, and her name was Elizabeth. Both were righteous in the eyes of God, observing all the commandments and ordinances of the Lord blamelessly. But they had no child, because Elizabeth was barren and both were advanced in years. Once when he was serving as priest in his division's turn before God, according to the practice of the priestly service, he was chosen by lot to enter the sanctuary of the Lord to burn incense. Then, when the whole assembly of the people was praying outside at the hour of the incense offering, the angel of the Lord appeared to him, standing at the right of the altar of incense. Zechariah was troubled by what he saw, and fear came upon him. But the angel said to him, "Do not be afraid, Zechariah, because your prayer has been heard. Your wife Elizabeth will bear you a son, and you shall name him John. And you will have joy and gladness, and many will rejoice at his birth, for he will be great in the sight of the Lord. He will drink neither wine nor strong drink. He will be filled with the Holy Spirit even from his mother's womb, and he will turn many of the children of Israel to the Lord their God. He will go before him in the spirit and power of Elijah to turn the hearts of fathers toward children and the disobedient to the understanding of the righteous, to prepare a people fit for the Lord." Then Zechariah said to the angel, "How shall I know this? For I am an old man, and my wife is advanced in years." And the angel said to him in reply, "I am Gabriel, who stand before God. I was sent to speak to you and to announce to you this good news. But now you will be speechless and unable to talk* until the day these things take place, because you did not believe my words, which will be fulfilled at their proper time."

Meanwhile the people were waiting for Zechariah and were amazed that he stayed so long in the sanctuary. But when he came out, he was unable to speak to them, and they realized that he had seen a vision in the sanctuary. He was gesturing to them but remained mute. Then, when his days of ministry were completed, he went home. After this time his wife Elizabeth conceived, and she went into seclusion for five months, saying, "So has the Lord done for me at a time when he has seen fit to take away my disgrace before others."

In Genesis 21:1-7, we also read about Sara and Abraham, who in their old age, became parents of Isaac.

Now the Lord was gracious to Sarah as he had said, and the Lord did for Sarah what he had promised. Sarah became pregnant and bore a son to Abraham in his old age, at the very time God had promised him. Abraham gave the name Isaac to the son Sarah bore him. When his son Isaac was eight days old, Abraham circumcised him, as God commanded him. Abraham was a hundred years old when his son Isaac was born to him. Sarah said, "God has brought me laughter, and everyone who hears about this will laugh with me." And she added, "Who would have said to Abraham that Sarah would nurse children? Yet I have borne him a son in his old age."

Yes, God is in "the business of making babies." Time and time again, I have received testimonies from couples who bore a baby or babies as an answer to prayers. Genesis 1:26-28, says,

Then God said: Let us make human beings in our image, after our likeness. Let them have dominion over the fish of the sea, the birds of the air, the tame animals, all the wild animals, and all the creatures that crawl on the earth. God created mankind in His image; in the image of God He created them; male and female He created them. God blessed them and God said to them: Be fertile and multiply; fill the earth and subdue it. Have dominion over the fish of the sea, the birds of the air, and all the living things that crawl on the earth.

In the following pages of this chapter are some of the testimonies I have received regarding healings of infertility and barrenness.

"I want to share my testimony with you today. The Lord has blessed me today.

I attended your service on November 14 in Sharjah, UAE. I came with my husband, hoping and believing for a blessing, which I am blessed with today.

You called for all of the couples who were planning for a baby, and I came out with my husband to receive my healing. Even before you could lay your hands over my husband, and me I was filled with the Holy Spirit, unable to control my weeping.

As you laid your hands over me, I fell down on the floor shivering in the Holy Spirit, and I knew at that very moment that God had blessed me with a baby. For nearly six months after the service, every month I would have hopes that I was pregnant, but the enemy would take control over me by bringing negative thoughts to my mind and there were times that I lost hope and faith in God.

Finally I took a firm stand and started rebuking the evil one in my life and I just remained cool and took things lightly. At that time, I told God to take control over me and guide me to the correct way. I believed that when you prayed over us, something very beautiful happened inside of me. I believed that God gave me this gift on my birthday, on April 13. And it was true. I was tested positive for being pregnant in the month of April. I have also heard of other couples who came to your service who are now expecting babies.

Since then, God is in control and he is taking care of all my troubles and worries. I really believe that God answers our prayers. I thank God for blessing me with this new life and also thank you and your ministry for the prayers.

As the scripture promises, 'Ask and it will be given to you; seek and you will find; knock and the door will be opened to you'" (Matthew 7:7).

—Love, Shal, Sharjah, UAE—

"Bob, this is Keith from St. Francis of Assisi in Henderson, NV. I have been the MC for the Life in the Spirit Seminars where you spoke. As per your request, I wanted to share with you the story about the conception of our baby. My wife, Karen, and I had our third child just two years ago. Because my youngest son's sisters were now at college, we wanted to have another child so that he would have a sibling to grow up with. We had two miscarriages following his birth and had been deeply saddened and worried that we would not be able to have another. However, during the Life in the Spirit Seminar you spoke at, you also prayed over my wife, Karen, for her to bear a child. A few months after that, she went in for a pregnancy test and found out she was pregnant. Based on the calculations from the doctor it appeared we conceived just following the day you prayed over her. Praise the Lord! Thank you for your prayers, and may the Lord bless you always!"

—Keith Henderson, NV—

"Hello. I just want to thank you and your wife for helping my husband and I. I had the opportunity to see you last year when you came to Ste Rose du Lac, MB (Canada). I had asked for prayers, as we have been trying to have a baby for four years and were beginning to give up hope. You and your wife prayed over us. You told us to be thankful to the Lord because 'He is doing some wonderful things for us.' I just found out that I was finally pregnant after four years of trying to have a baby. I am about four weeks into my pregnancy. Praise God, we are so happy, and we wanted to thank you from the bottom of our hearts. God bless you and your wife and your families! I was experiencing some bleeding and so I called you. You prayed for me for two days over the phone and, as of right now, the bleeding has stopped, Thank God, Praise You Jesus! I hope that you can come to Manitoba when the baby is born. I would like you to meet this angel that God has blessed us with. God is so good indeed.

I also want to share with you that I was healed through the Healing and Keeping Prayer that you wrote. I had a cyst on my hand for over a year. I said the Healing and Keeping prayer with faith that the cyst would be gone, and the next day I noticed that the cyst was totally gone. Thank you, Jesus, again. Thank you so much for all of your help. God bless!"

—*Debbie & Clayton, Manitoba, Canada*—

"My sister-in law had a miscarriage and she became very depressed and blamed herself for it. It took her awhile to get a little better emotionally, and then she became pregnant again. However, she had another miscarriage. She took the second miscarriage much harder than the first one and she was devastated emotionally and mentally. She felt that she could not bear a child again nor she could carry a pregnancy to full term. I took her to your Mass and healing service at St. Luke's Parish in Stockton.

Bob, when you prayed over her, you told her to give those two miscarried babies names and to forgive herself because the Lord wanted her to do so. How it is that you seemed to know about her and her mental and emotional conditions at that time still puzzles me. You then thanked the Lord for those babies and for welcoming them into His Kingdom and 'for giving them eternal rest.' Bob, I was amazed when you told my sister-in-law, through your word of knowledge from the Holy Spirit, that she had 'a curse to barrenness' in her life. You then broke the curse in the Name and by the Blood of Jesus, and you 'commanded' a blessing of fertility into her life by the Power of the Holy Spirit. I was equally amazed when you asked God to do unto my sister-in-law what He did to Sarah and to Elizabeth in their old age. We praised the Lord when you told us after you prayed over her that 'the Lord is doing great things for my sister-in-law, so don't worry, and keep on thanking and praising the Lord.' Bob, I'm happy to inform you that she got pregnant seven months after we

attended the Mass and healing service in St. Luke's Parish. Now she is holding a precious two-month-old healthy baby boy in her arms. For sure, he is a bundle of joy, and another precious gift from God to our family. We plan to come again during the Mass and healing service in your parish to give our testimony personally and to thank you for your prayers for her and for us. The impossible becomes possible with Jesus. He gives us what we cannot give to ourselves. Praise Jesus now and forever, Amen."
    —Rosario Caballero, Antioch, CA—

"Hi Bob, I would like to share with you some great news about my daughter. You prayed over my daughter, Delila, about four months ago during the Mass and healing service at St. Luke's Parish. She and her husband have been trying to have a baby for quite some time now. When you prayed over her, you asked the Lord to do to my daughter what He did to Sarah and to Elizabeth in spite of their old age. You also commanded her womb to be fertile in Jesus' Name. You also told my daughter to continue to trust in the goodness of the Lord and to praise Him all the time. We found out December 11 that she is about five or six weeks pregnant. Praise God. Thank you, Bob, for your prayers. My daughter's pregnancy is one of the best Christmas gifts from the Lord for our family ever. Everybody in the family is rejoicing. Thank you again, Brother Bob, for praying and spending time with people like us. God bless you and we will continue to pray for you and your family

and ministry. My family will come to St. Luke's Healing Service again to announce what God has done for us."
—Sophia Golde, Lathrop, CA—

"My daughter, Bianca Gabriel, whom you prayed over when you came into our house, was diagnosed with thyroid disease. Her doctor had prescribed medications for it, but she wasn't getting any better. She was told her hormones were not normal and there would be no way for her to get pregnant. Well, here is the great news: she is twenty-three weeks pregnant. Of course, she didn't initially even know about it. She wasn't taking any oral contraceptives because she thinks it is immoral, and she just thought she wouldn't be able to have any more children due to her thyroid condition. My husband, Roberto, thought at first that our daughter was just gaining weight. I took courage to ask our daughter Bianca whether or not she was pregnant. She said, 'Mom, I have no idea since I haven't had a menstrual cycle for over a year, and that was almost right after I had my first child.' She was puzzled and then took a home pregnancy test, which came back positive. The next day, she went in to see her doctor who ordered her to get some lab work done. And sure enough, the test confirmed that she was pregnant. They couldn't determine how far along she was due to her abnormal menstrual cycle, so they did an ultrasound, which I was able to attend. The doctor said the test shows she is having a little boy. She was twenty-two weeks and three days pregnant. Praise

the Lord, Jesus Christ for He made that miracle happen through your prayers. They ran the lab work and said that her thyroid level is normal and the test doesn't show any signs of a thyroid problem. This was puzzling to the doctors because she was earlier diagnosed to have thyroid abnormalities. My husband and I are thankful to God for all the wonderful things He has done in our lives. Thank you, Brother Bob, for praying over my daughter. Thank you for taking the time after your workshops in the church to come and pray for the family members in our home. My daughter was not only healed of her thyroid abnormalities, but we will also have a new addition to our family. Glory be to God! Our God is a "God full of pleasant surprises!"
—Irene, McMinville, OR—

∞

"Hi Brother Bob Canton. Good morning. I'm happy to share with you that since you've prayed over my wife and me to have a child during the Light of Jesus Community in Kerygma Feast, we have two beautiful kids. Thank God. He uses you as an instrument to bless married couples like us.

We had been trying for five years to conceive, but with no results until after you had prayed over us during the Kyregma Conference in the Ultra Stadium in Pasig, Rizal, Philippines. Six weeks after you prayed over us, we found out that my wife was over a month into the pregnancy of our first child. Every day, we thank the Lord for this big blessing in our lives. It was an instant answer to our prayers.

By the way, when are you coming back to the Philippines? Please let us know, okay? Everybody in our family has heard your name already and they want to meet you personally when you come again to our country."
—Rodrick S. Barrios, Quezon City, Philippines—

Prayer for Healing of Infertility and Barrenness

Lord Jesus, you are the author of life. In your Words in John 10:10, you said, "I have come to give you life and to have it abundantly." Use my spouse and me for procreation because according to God's Words, you want us to "be fertile and multiply." Lord Jesus, heal any or all of the causes of infertility; such as endometriosis, irregular ovulation, poor quantity and quality of eggs and/or sperm, polycystic ovarian syndrome, blocked or damaged fallopian tubes, or testicular injuries. In Jesus' mighty Name, and by the Blood of Jesus, I break and cancel out any curses to barrenness and infertility directed against my spouse and me and our bloodlines, and I render them null and void and ineffective. I speak of blessings of fertility to come forth unto my spouse and me in the holy Name of Jesus, through the mantle of Mary, the Immaculate Conception and the spouse of the Holy Spirit. Lord Jesus, remove any abnormal tissue from the abdominal pelvic cavity and cause the small follicles to develop into larger and mature follicles so that the eggs will be released properly. Come Holy Spirit and release the power to make the eggs and sperm fertilize into a normal and healthy fetus, in Jesus'

Name. Lord, thank you for your gift of love and your gift of life. I ask all of these in Jesus' powerful Name, through the intercession of Mary, the great Mother of God and St. Joseph, the husband of Mary. Amen.

CHAPTER EIGHTEEN

Miraculous Healings of the Heart, Lungs, and Kidneys

During His ministry here on Earth 2,000 years ago, Jesus spent a great deal of His time healing the sick. He is so opposed to sickness that He even healed some people during the Sabbath. We read in Luke 14:1-6,

> On a Sabbath He went to dine at the home of one of the leading Pharisees, and the people there were observing Him carefully. In front of Him there was a man suffering from dropsy. Jesus spoke to the scholars of the law and Pharisees in reply, asking, "Is it lawful to cure on the Sabbath or not?" But they kept silent; so He took the man and, after He had healed him, dismissed him. Then He said to them, "Who among you, if

your son or ox falls into a cistern, would not immediately pull him out on the Sabbath day?" But they were unable to answer His question.

Indeed, there is no sickness that Jesus cannot heal. The following testimonies can also attest to this fact.

"On February 2007, I was hospitalized for about nine days at the Cardiac Unit of Sarawak General Hospital, Kuching, with breathing difficulties and fluid in my lungs. An ultrasound scan and MRI tests showed that one heart artery was partially hardened, a second artery was 100 percent blocked and a third artery was 90 percent blocked. The heart specialists advised surgery if I wanted to live longer.

However, my kidneys were also not in good health; tests showed that my kidneys had shrunk by some 20 percent, and surgery could not be performed even though my condition demanded immediate attention and surgery. For the same reason, the doctors also did not dare to do an angiogram on me.

These problems began at the end of February 2006 after my election as Superior General of the Congregation, the 10th Chapter.

On the morning of May 9, 2008, a friend of mine took me to the Bob Canton workshop and I arrived late, at about 10:30 A.M. in the morning, when the sessions had already started. Just as my friend and I walked in the door at the back of the hall, Brother Bob received a word of knowledge and said that the Lord wants to heal someone present with congestive heart failure, and that the Lord wanted to give this person a new heart. He went on to say that this person was hospitalized recently.

I immediately went forward to claim my healing. When Bob prayed for me, I fell to the floor and rested in the Spirit and I heard Bob saying, 'God is giving her a new heart!' Whilst I was down on the floor, I felt a slight pain on the left part of my chest that went upwards to my left shoulder. I sensed that my breathing became heavy. When the Emmaus Healing Team members were praying the Divine Mercy Novena, I felt the pain subside slowly and I could breathe normally again.

I was told that during the time when I was resting in the Spirit, a sister from the Emmaus Community had a vision of surgery taking place and saw a heart being taken out and replaced by a new heart and the artery being stitched together.

The good Lord has indeed given a new heart to me. Since that morning, I have felt very well. Whereas before I was not able to climb stairs and had to sleep in a room on the ground floor at the convent, I now can climb two flights of stairs, carrying my bags, without difficulty. I no longer feel breathless or short of breath. My complexion is now healthy; whereas before I used to look pale. I used to feel giddy and was fearful of traveling alone as I did not feel well and was worried I could faint anytime. All of that is gone and the doctors recently told me that my kidneys are practically functioning normally again!

I praise and thank God for this divine intervention and healing. God loves you!"

—*Sister Adriana Tiong, Sarawak, Kuching, Malaysia—*

"I will attempt to be brief in my testimony. And I pray that our Lord Jesus Christ shall help me word it in a way to inspire anyone who reads it with hope, faith and love for Jesus. I am sixty-three years old. On March 8, 2012, I had a severe heart attack, which resulted in my having to undergo quintuple coronary bypass surgery, after which I spent six weeks in a cardiac rehabilitation therapy facility in order to strengthen my heart.

Needless to say, this entire experience was a difficult challenge, taxing me physically, mentally, emotionally and spiritually. The ensuing heart tests indicated a diagnosis of congestive heart failure, which required me to take diuretic medicine to help eliminate the fluid build-up in my body. This meant that my heart was not strong enough to help eliminate the retained fluid, which could fill up in my lungs and keep me from breathing. Whenever I did not take the medicine, I would notice the swelling in my legs and feet and, ultimately, shortness of breath in my lungs. Obviously, this meant I would continue to, and always have to, use the diuretic.

In October 2012, I was invited by my friend, Bob, a very devoted Catholic, to attend your healing service on October 9, 2012, at St. Edward the Confessor in Clifton Park, NY. Your service and sermon were very inspirational to me. Even though I could feel the presence of Jesus, I was having my doubts as to whether or not Jesus would heal me in any way through you. But as I stood with the gathering of others around you, praying with them for healing, I could undoubtedly feel Jesus' powerful presence as each person fell back into the arms of the catchers. When you turned to face me, you asked for what condition I needed healing, and I spoke the words "congestive heart failure." You placed your hand in front of my chest, and as you began to pray you tapped lightly on my chest. Immediately, I was overcome by the Holy Spirit's pouring into my body, overtaking me as I unintentionally, without thought, fell backward into the arms of the catchers. Laying there, eyes closed, I was feeling the warm and peaceful presence of the Holy Spirit. Sometimes I think this feeling of the Holy Spirit in me that evening is indescribable to anyone who hasn't yet experienced it. I am so thankful to you, and for the mercy and love from Jesus!

Now for the best part (actually, all of it is the best). After that night, I started noticing that physically, I felt less of a need to take the diuretic medicine. So I started experimenting with not taking it. Within days, I found that there was no swelling in my legs or ankles, no shortness of breath, and no need to take the medicine! This was okayed by my doctor when I saw him a few weeks later and after he had performed tests on me. Ever since then, I have not taken the medication. I just don't need to take it anymore. Praise Jesus Christ! I thank God for you. And I thank God for my friend, Bob, for inviting me and being present in prayer while you prayed for me. Bob, in closing, I would like to say: May God continue to bless and protect you in your ministry and travels. I will pray for you. Thank you so much."

—*Patrick Cassady, Clifton Park, NY*—

"I had just had an insurance requisite physical when you called me in my office to discuss the Alliance of Filipino Catholic Charismatic Prayer Communities' issues, and you asked me how I was doing. It was one of those down days for me then, because the insurance examiner found that I had an irregular heartbeat; a shock to me as I have always had a healthy cardiovascular system. You interrupted our conversation by praying for me and for my health over the phone. Honestly, I was skeptical. But at a follow-up exam a week later, my heartbeat showed that it had become as regular as usual, without medication or change in dietary, exercise, or leisure habits. Praise the Lord and thank you for your concern and your prayers."

—*Narciso Albarracin, Jr., M.D., Columbus, OH*—

"I and some friends of mine came down from Lodi to attend the Mass and Healing Service at St. Luke's Parish in Stockton. Our main intention was to bring our friend who was dying from cancer to the Healing Service.

Minutes before the people were all to go to the members of the healing teams for prayers, Bob Canton stopped us and said, 'I received a word of knowledge that the Lord Jesus is healing someone who has a heart problem known as mitral valve problem. This person has a shortness of breath and an extreme low blood pressure. The Lord Jesus Christ is healing you now by the power of the Holy Spirit.' I literally jumped for joy. Bob was exactly describing my physical condition. I've had this problem for eight years. My doctor has tried all kinds of medications but to no avail. I used to feel so tired that I couldn't even do simple household chores such as washing and cleaning the windows. I used to have shortness of breath by walking even a short distance. It is difficult to live a life when you can't function well like a healthy, normal person.

After Bob called out this healing, I felt like there was a sudden surge of energy that went through my body. There was a knowing deep inside me that I was healed and I kept on praising and thanking God for it. Three days later, I woke up feeling so refreshed and so "new." I started doing household chores without any problem. I even washed and cleaned my windows without experiencing shortness of breath, and my husband had noticed it right away. I had also started walking longer distances with no problem at

all. My doctor told me that my heart was doing good and my blood pressure was almost back to normal. I'm doing normal physical activities without restriction whatsoever. I came to the Healing Service to pray for my friend's healing. The Lord also saw my needs and He touched me with His healing and loving hands. We should always trust in His love for us for nothing at all is impossible for Him."
—Barbara Tasse, Lodi, CA—

"I can't remember if I ever gave you a testimony about the healing of my brother, Clayton. In August 2006, I had called you for prayers because my brother, a doctor, had been taken to hospital with problems in the legs - blockages - and needed bypass surgery, perhaps quadruple bypass surgery, to be performed on him. He was in the hospital and rehab for a few months.

With myself as proxy, you prayed for Clayton several times. It was felt that he might not be able to perform surgeries again because of his feet. But God is a God of miracles and Clayton was healed and back to performing surgeries and delivering babies. His heart is in good condition and there has been no damage to his heart from the previous blockage. Late last year he had a problem with his leg and was hospitalized. I called you immediately when I learned of this and you prayed for Clayton using me as proxy once again. You also said that the Lord said that there would be no surgery. The problem would be fixed by other methods. I did not tell them anything.

A few days later, I received a call that the doctors would not operate and that his condition would be treated with medication. Praise God, he is well again; back to driving and performing surgeries. God is to be praised for His miracles. These experiences have brought him much closer to the Lord. Please continue to lift him and his family up in prayers.

I would also like to give thanks and praise for my own healing, that of my thyroid condition. I had a complete thyroidectomy in March 2006. I had been previously healed of suspected cancer after a first surgery in November 2003 - this was confirmed by a full body scan in August 2007. You had prayed with me several times before the scan. However, the thyroglobulin antibody level was elevated from -2 to 3.4 and also the thyroglobulin level.

The Lord directed me to a new endocrinologist who carefully studied my case, which she considered unique (this was my third thyroid surgery; I had one in Guyana in 1973, then the two here in California - the gland kept regenerating itself). She prescribed a new treatment and ordered another blood test after two months. You had prayed over me the night before the blood test, speaking to the thyroglobulin levels. God is good. I have just received my results. Both levels have gone down to normal, where they should be for someone without a thyroid gland, and cancer free."

—Joan Dundas, Glendale, CA—

"*Thank you again, Brother Bob, for praying over me yesterday. I called you because the serum creatinine in my blood test was 1.62 (normal is 0.6 to 1.27). I was having dizzy spells for the past week so I called my cardiologist and he ordered routine blood tests. I have a history of cardiac catheterization with stent placement from ten years ago, and I have had multiple exposures to intravenous dye. Two months ago, I was having abdominal pains and numerous tests were done again, including an abdominal CT scan with intravenous contrast. Before that test, I had a serum creatinine of 1.26, which was high-normal.*

Anyway, with an elevation of my serum creatinine to 1.62, I was concerned. I consulted a renal specialist who ordered so many tests, including a kidney ultrasound. His diagnosis was acute renal failure. I was really scared, knowing what my patients on dialysis have to undergo (I even asked my wife if she would be willing to give me one of her kidneys!).

Last night, my wife and I went to Adoration (Blessed Sacrament), as that was our scheduled date with our Lord every week, and this morning we went to Mass and received Him in the Holy Eucharist. I asked our Lord to have His Blood flow through my heart and kidneys, since He was there in me. I then went to the hospital and had my blood and urine tests done.

Praise God! My serum creatinine is 1.16 (normal) and my urine test is normal.

I thank the Lord for His goodness and love for those who love Him. I thank you, Brother Bob, again, for your

time and kindness for those who seek your help to pray for them in the Name of Jesus. What you said after you prayed with me was really true. You said, 'The Lord is telling me to tell you, Ray, not to be afraid, because everything will be okay.'
    —Dr. Ray Caparros, Millerville, MD—

Your ministries are God sent! I don't know how many times I've had spells with my heart. My cousin in Florida sent me your Healing and Keeping Prayer. I have been praying that prayer every day. One cannot believe the power of it.

I had two spells with my heart a week apart. My family doctor sent me to a heart specialist and he had me do test after test. I started praying your prayer just before my last set of testing. The results were unbelievable. No blocked arteries! Thank you, Jesus!"
    —Betty J. Sullivan, Cincinnati, OH—

"I was suffering from deep congestion in my lungs, and I was having trouble breathing, so my doctor decided to take an X-ray to see the extent and location of the congestion. The result of the X-ray indicated that I had a collapsed lung. Besides that problem, I also had a kidney stone. The doctor called it a stag horn kidney stone. The kidney was not infected, so my doctor advised to leave it alone. That was fine with me because I was not looking

forward to a kidney operation. I didn't think too much about it until I was on an extended business trip to Japan and Taiwan. The thought of having an attack on board the airplane or in a foreign country caused me to resolve to see my doctor upon my arrival back in Stockton.

It was at the Children of God Prayer Community's prayer meeting, at St. Luke's Parish, that Bob Canton announced through the word of knowledge that the Lord Jesus was healing someone with a kidney stone. I did not think too much about it, at first, but then I thought, that could be me who was healed of that ailment. I made an appointment with my doctor the following week and I told him that there was a possibility that my kidney ailment had been cured. He then ordered an X-ray of my kidney to be taken. Upon reviewing the first set of X-rays, the doctor informed me that he could not see the kidney stone, but that he wanted to take a series of X-rays of a stronger magnitude to be sure.

It was after the second set of X-rays that the radiologist explained that he could not see any evidence of a kidney stone. My family doctor also explained that he could no longer see the stone and that it must have dissolved. Deep inside me, I know that the Lord Jesus must have dissolved the stag horn stone, which I understand to be a big one. I am convinced that the prayers of the Children of God Prayer Community and their devotion to prayer has brought about this healing and many other healings of various kinds. I also thank them for warmly welcoming my wife and me to their prayer meetings. Most of all,

Miraculous Healings of the Heart, Lungs, and Kidneys

I give thanks and praise to our Lord Jesus Christ, our Divine Healer."

—Bob Chinchiolo, Stockton, CA—

"I want to thank the Lord for the miracle He has given us through Brother Bob Canton. This miracle has enabled my sick mother to breathe without oxygen. Let me tell you the story about my Mom.

Three months ago, my mother's health started to deteriorate. Her doctor gave her all the medication she needed plus oxygen to sleep. Instead of getting better, she became worse and she needed oxygen twenty-four hours around the clock. Without inhaled oxygen, her blood oxygen saturation drops to 46 percent or lower, which is very low and dangerous. This continued for the last three months and she has been confined to her room. She used the restroom with much difficulty, getting easily short of breath.

When my husband told me about the prayer meeting that was to be held on Saturday, April 14, 2007, I was worried about how I would tell my boss, as I would be missing work. But, praise the Lord, she had no problem with it. I then told my sister to have my mother ready by 8:00 A.M. on Saturday morning because we were going to bring her to a Healing Mass. On Friday I needed to buy oxygen, but I ran out of time. On Saturday morning when I called the oxygen company, they said they were closed and I told them, 'Please. I need the oxygen so I can bring my Mom to a Healing Mass,' so the lady told me to bring forty dollars cash and they would give me two tanks. When I went to get the money from my bank my PIN number did not work. It looked like everything was going wrong. Thank God that the bank was open. I entered just with my ATM card, I had no identification on me, and I went to the teller. I told her I needed money to buy my Mom oxygen and she asked for identification. I told her, 'Sorry, I left it in my car.' She asked me a few questions and then gave me the money. I ran to get the oxygen and went home to pick up my Mom. It was very close to 11:30 A.M., and I found no traffic on my way home or heading to the prayer meeting. When we left the house, my mother gave great effort just to go down the stairs. I told my sister to put the oxygen setting on 3 liters. We forgot to put the oxygen back to 2 liters (oxygen in the tank will only last 4 hours at a setting of 2 liters). In the middle of the prayer meeting, I noticed that the oxygen tank was almost empty. I said, 'Lord, if things get worse from here I will have to get my Mom admitted to University Medical Center.'

When Brother Bob Canton prayed over my mother, he asked to remove the oxygen tank. I felt scared but I did what he told me. She became very short of breath, especially when he asked her to walk. My mother stated afterwards: 'I was gasping for air and I didn't know how I was able to walk back and forth.' Then she sat down and started to relax. Color came back to her face and she started to breathe slowly and more calmly. She was able to go without oxygen for almost fifteen minutes without struggle. The prayer meeting continued and more prayers were said over her. She fainted and when she woke up she said, 'I cannot breathe!' She was lying flat on the floor. We put her up and she recovered very quickly without the oxygen. The prayer meeting finished, and my mother walked to the food section without oxygen. She ate, and we stayed in the room for another thirty minutes. We left, and she was walking, pushing her wheelchair without oxygen. Halfway to the door she became short of breath, so we put the inhaler on and she recovered very fast. We left, and in the car she said, 'I feel like I have the oxygen on and I can take deep breaths.' We were very happy, and my sister and I started to say, 'Amen, thank you, Jesus!' I was so happy I brought her to eat ice cream! We arrived home around 9:00 P.M. She still was without oxygen. She sat down in my family room for ten minutes. Then she went upstairs. She did get short of breath, but she recovered promptly. We checked her oxygenation level and she was at 72 percent after five hours without oxygen. She said, 'I feel very good.' We started to thank the Lord for such a blessing. She slept with the oxygen on last night and when she woke up her oxygen saturation, with the setting at just 1 liter, was at 80 percent. Before, it would be in the low fifties. Then she took off the oxygen and spent the whole day without it, and still her oxygenation level did not drop below 75 percent. Walking to the bathroom did not get her short of breath.

I called Brother Bob at 9:50 P.M. and I left a message of gratitude. Then the one who became short of breath was me. He called me back and started to pray on the phone with me. After I hung up, I noticed my respiration became settled and I was feeling better.

Thank you, Lord Jesus, for the favors I have received. Thanks for giving my mother a second chance to live! I beg the Lord Jesus Christ to keep Brother Bob free of any harm and to give him health and strength to keep going around the world helping people as he helped my family. God bless you and your family, Brother Bob Canton. My Mom's oxygen saturation is 74 percent after fifteen hours with no oxygen."

—*Martha Valles, Las Vegas, NV*—

"*October 18, 2004, I was rushed to Rashid Hospital, Dubai, UAE, because of breathing difficulties. I thought it was because of my hypertension, but I was diagnosed with having a fibrosis and my lungs were not functioning normally anymore. They were not absorbing oxygen to supply my body, which means that my body oxygen supply was only 50 percent normal. I was advised by the doctors to use an oxygen concentrator to supply my body with the right amount of oxygen. And I would have to use it for eighteen hours every day. The doctor told me not to do any housework and that I must have complete rest every day. After a year, I was prescribed to reduce the oxygen concentrator to sixteen hours each day. But all this time I was continuously praying for healing. I never stopped praising and thanking Him, and we continue our services with Couples for Christ as Chapter 2 head servants.*

Finally, God answered my prayer. December 7 to 9, 2008 we attended the first Gulf Catholic Charismatic Conference in Abu Dhabi, UAE. As it was a three-day conference, I had to bring my oxygen tank with me. It was during the healing session that Brother Bob Canton declared there was somebody in the audience who was suffering from lung sickness, and that the Lord was healing that person. Then afterwards we went to see Bob Canton, and he prayed over me. I felt something very cold in my back, followed by something very warm, as if my body was on fire. I felt better afterwards, and we went home to Dubai that day. Then my husband was very surprised that night when I did not use my oxygen concentrator in my sleep. Before that day, I have had to have oxygen even during my sleeping time. A few days later, I started to do my household chores and I started living normally again. My doctor was very surprised that my lungs and the oxygen level have returned to normal again. I thank God for answering my prayers. Until now, I always thank, praise and glorify Him, and I still pray for healing not for me but for other sick people. Praise God. Alleluia. Thank you, Brother Bob, for your prayers for me."
—Mel E., Dubai, UAE—

"I had been suffering from allergy and asthma attacks for at least fifteen years. I have had coughing spasms and wheezing plus sore throat, runny nose, and clogged up ears. I had been

taking some medications, but my allergies continued to bother me. I was resigned to have asthma and allergies all my life.

When I went up to San Damiano Retreat House in Danville, CA, to attend the Healing service that evening, I had little expectations that I would receive a healing. In fact, when I arrived at the retreat house, I had a few allergy attacks.

During the Holy Sacrifice of the Mass, I asked the Lord Jesus to heal me of my physical illness. This was what Fr. Sebastian Drake encouraged us to do during his homily, to receive the healing and loving touch of Jesus.

After the Mass, Bob Canton announced the healings that were taking place using the gift of the word of knowledge. When he announced that the Lord Jesus was healing a woman who has been suffering from asthma and allergy attacks, I knew he was talking about me. When I stood up to acknowledge the healing, he asked me to run around the room as fast as I could. As I was running around the room, I felt a beautiful presence of the Lord Jesus. When I stopped running, I had noticed to my amazement that I wasn't wheezing and I was breathing normally. I haven't had any allergy or asthma attacks since then. Also, I used to have pains in my left knee for a long time. That pain also disappeared that very night.

I consider what happened to me as a miracle not only because of the healings that I received but because I encountered the Lord Jesus and I felt His awesome presence that evening. That experience has made me closer to Him every day. I thank the Lord for loving me and for letting me know that He answers prayers."

—Julie Ashlemen, Hayward, CA—

Prayer for Healing of the Lungs

Lord, in your words, you say that you formed my innermost being; you knitted me in my mother's womb. Praise you, because I am wonderfully made; wonderful are your works! I ask you now, Lord, to heal my body, especially my lungs. In Jesus' Name, I command the cause or causes of lung problems such as COPD, pulmonary embolism, cystic fibrosis, emphysema, asthma, inflammation of bronchus and alveoli, bronchitis, pneumonia, pulmonary edema, acute pulmonary distress, pulmonary hypertension, pleural effusion, neuromuscular disorder, pneumoconiosis, and other unknown causes to be healed completely. Lord Jesus, I saturate by faith all the parts of my lungs with your most precious Blood so that my lungs will function normally. Lord, I ask for brand new lungs because you are the God of the impossible. I also apply by faith your powerful healing touch into my lungs, the same touch with which you touched the blind, the deaf, the leprous, the lame, and the dead while you were still walking on this Earth. Thank you, Jesus, for hearing and granting this prayer. Amen.

Prayer for Healing of Heart Diseases

Lord, touch also my heart. I also apply by faith your most precious Blood into all the parts of my heart, the tissues and muscles, the valves and arteries and blood vessels and veins. I command the cause or causes of heart ailments such as coronary artery disease, angina, diabetes, congestive heart failure, high blood pressure, atrial fibrillation, irregular heartbeats, heart valve diseases, cardiomyopathy and other unknown causes and I command the build-up of plaques and blood clots in my arteries to be dissolved and to be completely healed in the mighty Name of Jesus. In Jesus' Name, I command the stiffening of the heart muscles to be healed, and the heart muscle and the electrical conduction system to be strengthened. I command the heart to deliver oxygen-rich blood into my entire body, and the abnormal accumulation of fluid in the kidneys and in other parts of the body to disappear completely, in Jesus' precious Name. I speak of the divine cleansing of my vascular system and all the systems of my body, and the creative miracles of a brand new heart. Thank you, Lord Jesus, because in you there is always healing and wholeness. I thank you and I praise your Holy Name. Amen.

Prayer for Healing of Kidney Diseases

Lord Jesus, it is your will for me to have healthy, great, and normal-functioning kidneys. I ask you now to saturate my kidneys with your precious healing blood, the same blood that you shed on the Cross at Calvary. I also apply by faith your loving and powerful healing hands unto my kidneys so that my kidneys will be recreated and become new again, for nothing at all is impossible for you. Lord Jesus, I believe that you are a God of creative miracles and all glory and honor belong to you. In Jesus' Name, I command the cause or possible causes of kidney malfunctions or disease such as diabetes, high blood pressure, lupus, polycystic kidney disease, urinary tract infection, inflammation in the tiny filters within the kidneys, urinary tract obstructions and malfunctions, urinary long-term exposure to some medications or chemicals to be healed completely and not to affect my kidneys anymore. I command any kidney stone to be dissolved and to be turned into powder so that I can pass it without pain or discomfort or to disappear completely in Jesus' mighty Name. Divine Master Healer, cause my kidneys to function normally by the power of the Holy Spirit. I command the pancreas to produce insulin in my body and the blood sugar to go down to normal and my immunity system to function normally without causing any harm or damage to my kidneys in the mighty Name of Jesus. I thank you, Lord, and I believe that your divine power is touching me now to heal and rejuvenate my kidneys. Praise your Name, my Lord Jesus, my Savior and Healer. Amen.

CHAPTER NINETEEN

Miraculous Healings of Various Types of Diseases

I n this chapter, I would like to include testimonies of various types of healing done in the beautiful Name of Jesus, the Master Healer, by the power of the Holy Spirit.

All of these testimonies indicate that healing is an answer to prayer. As I mentioned in an earlier chapter of this book, one of the purposes of the Healing Ministry is to draw people to the Lord and to His Kingdom, and to relieve human suffering.

In John 21:25, God's words state

> There are also many other things that Jesus did, but if these were to be described individually, I do not think the whole world would contain the books that would be written.

Jesus went around to all the towns and villages, teaching in their synagogues, proclaiming the Gospel of the kingdom, and curing every disease and illness. At the sight of the crowds, His heart was moved with pity for them because they were troubled and abandoned,* like sheep without a shepherd. Then He said to His disciples, "The harvest is abundant but the laborers are few; so ask the Master of the Harvest to send out laborers for His harvest." (Matthew 9:35-38)

The following testimonies point out that there is no sickness that Jesus cannot heal. There is no limit to His love, no limit to His power to heal, no limit to His Kingship and sovereignty. Below is a cornucopia of healing that indicates, once again, the undying love of God for His people.

"I would like my testimonies to be told for God's glory because I am so thankful to God for answering my prayers. You see, my daughter-in-law had a very difficult pregnancy. When she was around four months pregnant, after many tests such as sonogram and others, her doctor told her that the baby she was carrying was dead. Believe me, it was a shock to all of us, and we cried and cried. Then we started to pray your healing prayer card and we asked the Lord

for a miracle. The doctor told my daughter-in-law that the dead fetus in her womb had to be removed because it might cause blood poisoning. The night before the doctor's scheduled procedure to remove the fetus, we called you for prayers. I remember quite well when you spoke life into the dead fetus three times in the Name of Jesus and you commanded the dead fetus to live. The following day in the hospital, the doctors told my daughter that they detected heartbeats in the fetus, so the procedure was cancelled. My grandchild is alive. You could not imagine the happiness that we felt. I thank the Lord from the bottom of my heart for this miracle.

Five months later, in February, my daughter-in-law delivered a healthy, beautiful little girl. Her second name is 'Milagros,' meaning a 'miracle.' Without question, she is a miracle baby.

My second testimony is about my son. He was diagnosed with Type 2 diabetes. Since he was very, very sick, he decided to see his doctor. His blood sugar was 800. His doctor prescribed him four insulin pills a day. We tried to call you many times for prayers, but you were out of the country. We kept on praying your healing prayer card for my son. His blood sugar has gone down quite a bit and now he only needs one insulin pill a day. He is getting much, much better. The Lord hears our prayers for sure. Please include him also in your prayers.

Thank you very much for your help. We are praying for you and your ministry every day. May the Lord bless you always."
—Soc Reyes, WI—

"I would like to tell you the details as to what happened to my sister Lucille to be able to testify how powerful and almighty God has been! My sister, Lucille, who was with us in our recent pilgrimage to Israel, collapsed in the early morning of last June 14. She was brought to the hospital via ambulance and was in a comatose state. The doctors who treated her at the emergency room said that she was unresponsive, and she remained in a coma for the next three days. The doctors diagnosed her condition as encephalitis. Since I had just left her in Hawaii to come back to Manila, I was in a panic and state of shock knowing that I had just spoken to her the night before this happened. The only thing on my mind was to find a way to help her out with her condition. This led me to call you in California to ask for assistance in prayers. You responded by praying over her on the telephone last June 17. You said that the Lord was healing her and that she should recover. You did not have any doubt whatsoever and you told me to keep on praying and thanking the Lord. Although I was still worried about my sister, deep inside I felt a little bit consoled by what you said.

It was such a miracle that she opened her eyes the next morning, although disoriented, and she did not know what had happened to her; she was very conscious of who she was and knew what her name was. I knew that this was the work of God through your action. We received a blessing from Him! My sister is now okay!

I would like to thank you and express deep appreciation for your help. You were the messenger from heaven to us!"

—Hilaria Golamco, Manila, Philippines—

"Dear Brother and Sisters, before I attended the healing prayer, I was diagnosed with a kidney impairment. After I heard this diagnosis, I was determined to attend the Healing Mass at Blessed Sacrament in Kuching, Sarawak, Malaysia. After the Healing Mass, I tried to walk down the altar to be prayed over but someone stopped me along the way. However, Brother Bob Canton announced that someone's kidney was being healed by the Lord. When I went for a medical checkup, the doctor told me that my kidneys are back to normal. He said that my kidneys are like brand new. The result of the ultrasound scanning amazed me with God's wonders and His healing touch on me. I'm grateful that I am free from the torture and the pain that caused me to feel down. Thanks to the Lord Jesus Christ!

Thou shall believe in Him,
Thou will be done,
Do not test him,
Believe in Him
And always remain so.

Praise be the great Lord. He will heal anyone and will always be there to help the needy to be free from sorrows and pain in their life."

—Christopher H., Kuching, Sarawak, Malaysia—

"My name is Ann Fernandez. I had a hyperthyroid problem and was taking medications for a long time. I attended the Mass and Healing service last February 16, 2013, at St. Luke's Parish in Stockton. I had heard about it from my cousin who lives in Stockton. He said that many had been healed by attending the Mass and Healing service at your place. During the Service you announced, 'someone was getting healed of a thyroid problem by the Lord.' I came up for prayers, and you and your wife prayed with me. You told me to 'Rejoice because Jesus was releasing His healing power unto me.' Then, I fell down on the floor. I felt 'warmth' all over my body.

I saw the thyroid specialist four days later, and on February 20, he ordered a blood test for me. The next day, February 21, the doctor told me to stop taking the thyroid medications. He said that the medications are no longer necessary because the tests show normal results.

I am now rejoicing as you have told me to do. I feel much closer to the Lord. All my family members and friends are really amazed.

Many of my friends are coming to Stockton for the next Mass and Healing service on March 16.

I thank God for his grace and mercy.
　　　　　　　　—Ann Fernandez, Fairfield, CA—

"On September 21 and 22, 2012, the Lord made it possible for me to attend the Spiritual Warfare Conference led by Robert Canton of Robert Canton Ministries. This conference took place at the Holy Trinity Parish in Spruce Grove, Alberta. On the second day and right before lunch, Robert at one point said that there was someone in the room that was suffering from panic attacks to the point of paralysis. Since nobody came forward, and after Robert waited a little longer for a response, he finally said: 'That person is here, and that person is now healed!'

I didn't believe Robert was referring to me until, suddenly, right after he uttered these words, I experienced a warm feeling that started in my feet and slowly made its way up my calf muscles. Confused by this sudden occurrence, I then realized that Robert had been speaking about me all along.

You see, I had been suffering from an undiagnosed condition that started in 2000, but got worse in 2002. At the time, I was in school at the College of St. Joseph, VT doing my undergraduate studies and playing competitive basketball for my school. It was in the summer of 2002 that this condition, which I will describe shortly, got worse. It even prevented me from playing my last year of college basketball right after winning in the first conference championship in school history, and while I was captain of the team.

What I would experience in my worst state was my muscles seizing up to the point where I could neither walk nor get out of bed. My muscles felt so stiff that simply moving them would cause tremendous pain. No medicine, no pain-killers, no muscle relaxers helped. The only thing I could do would be to lie down and simply wait for the 'storm' to pass.

In addition to that, constant fatigue was something that had become part of my daily life. Fatigue and muscles seizing up, those two went hand-in-hand and there was nothing that I could do. The only thing I could do was rest as much as possible and lay down. I couldn't walk properly because my muscles had lost their flexibility. I would naturally do my best to walk properly and hide it from the people that saw me, but every step, every swing of the arm, every attempt to sit or get up would trigger discomforting pain. It felt as if my muscles had limited flexibility, a reduced range of motion, coupled with stiffness. Doing normal day-to-day movements would take them out of their range of motion, thus, triggering excruciating pain. These occurrences were random and would come and go, and some days would be worse than others. One day, I would be okay, the next, it would not be a good day. But it would never fail that when I was under a tremendous amount of stress, these 'attacks' would surface and I would be affected for a couple of days or even a week.

My muscles have seized up to the point where I would fall to the ground and be unable to move, in excruciating pain. And there have been several times when I needed someone to help me walk, get out of bed, and even help me move my limbs because I couldn't do it myself because of the pain. They would help me, for instance, to lift and extend my legs on a couch or bed after sitting.

On the days where I could move around, this condition still made its presence felt with a sudden painful muscle spasm or twitch to a lesser degree. I had gone to several doctors and hospitals both in the United States and Canada, undergone a variety of tests, and nothing had been conclusive. These tests included blood work, a heart exam, nerve tests and CAT scans (CT scans). All the doctors would say was that based on all the tests that have been done up till now, it appeared that I had a healthy body and they had no definitive answers for me.

Due to this lingering condition, over the years I have missed classes in college, work days during my professional career, had to leave work early or come in to work late, and even take leaves of absence.

After Robert Canton announced the healing, I could feel that this gentle fire was in specific areas of my back: my lower back and shoulder blades. It was as if it was targeting specific areas of my body that were damaged and needed healing.

And yes, that day, I was healed by our Lord Jesus Christ through the power of the Holy Spirit.

An hour later, when the conference resumed, I could feel the warm feeling in my forearms moving from my elbow to my wrist, as if I was being scanned.

Late that afternoon, I could feel it in my right leg below my knee, with the intensity of this fire being heightened a notch. The strange thing I noticed about the fire is that it felt like a fire. I felt all the effects of a fire without the burning. This gentle fire had been working on my body non-stop since Robert said that I had been healed.

And following Robert's advice, I've read the Healing and Keeping Prayer every morning to ensure the healing effect of the Holy Spirit continues to work on me. A week and two days have gone by since the conference and I still feel this gentle fire in my body. Now, I feel relieved, full of energy again, and that I am myself again. September 22, 2012 is a day that I'll never forget. Thank you, Robert, for giving me my life back. Praise the Lord.

Also thank you, Chita, for praying for my family. Your prayers have helped bring peace in our home since my sisters don't suffer from spiritual nightmares as frequently as they used to. And Robert, they've also been reading your Spiritual Warfare Prayers before going to sleep and it has quickly made a difference in their lives. They have better dreams now.

By the way, I've shared the Healing and Keeping Prayer with relatives, friends and those I believe will find it helpful. And will continue to do so. Thank you for everything, Robert and Chita. May God continue to bless you and protect you in your travels."

—*Tadumi, Edmonton, Alberta, Canada*—

"My left shoulder had been bothering me for two to three years. I'd had a cortisone shot, and been to a physiotherapist where they did all kinds of therapy, including acupuncture. I was being sent to a surgeon, but needed an MRI for that visit. When the report came back, it said I had four things wrong

with my shoulder: I had osteoarthritis, a pinched nerve, and two separate tears in the tendons.

During the Friday evening of Bob Canton's talk about Setting the Captives Free in Spruce Grove/Stony Plain, Alberta, he stopped himself and said, 'Someone here has a sore shoulder. Circle your shoulder a few times and then stick your hand straight up in the air because in Jesus' Name it is healed.' I had been circling my shoulder, and was stunned when I was able to stick it straight up! I hadn't been able to get my arm up past my head (in fact, it was difficult to do my hair with that hand). Praise be to God My shoulder is healed!

I thank our God for His love, which enabled me to hear about the Conference, to be able to attend, and for blowing the embers of my faith into a bonfire once again. I pray for my brothers and sisters in Christ here at St. Gabriel's Parish in Athabasca Alberta. May St. Gabriel, our patron, continue to bring the message of the love and power of the name 'Jesus' to our community. And may God, in His Love and Mercy, give us the ears to hear and the open hearts to grab hold of that message and pass it on. I pray also that the Lord will continue to use Bob Canton to heal His people in Jesus' Name. Amen."

—Gord Hunt, Athabasca, Alberta, Canada—

"We had a wonderful time with Bob Canton and his wife from the April 18-22 in Esbjerg, Denmark, where I am the parish priest. Jesus was working miracles through their ministry. Here are some of the many testimonies:

Miraculous Healings of Various Types of Diseases

Deacon Kaare Nielsen sent this e-mail from Copenhagen to Esbjerg: A lady was brought into hospital in Lyngby where Bob had been ministering. This lady was struck by a blood clot. A Danish Catholic priest, Father Brodersen, went to see her and brought the Healing and Keeping Prayer of Bob Canton, and he prayed the prayer with the lady, who was healed instantly. Praise God.

During one of the healing masses in Esbjerg, a sixty-year-old man, Vagn Konradsen, was healed from a cataract when Bob laid his hands on his eyes. Now he sees perfectly. Praise God.

A young Vietnamese boy, nineteen years of age, Jimmy Nguyen, was resting in the spirit after being prayed over for a fractured shoulder. He was meant to go in for an operation. The following day he stopped taking painkillers ,because the pain had left and the shoulder is now perfectly well. Praise God.

A Vietnamese lady, Anna Nguyen, sixty-one years of age was prayed over for a hearing problem. For ten years she had been wearing hearing aids and after being prayed over, her hearing was restored and she is not using hearing aids anymore. Praise God.

A Polish lady, Katarina, was prayed over for a back problem and for migraines and problems with her lungs. After being prayed over, she could breathe normally, and the pain had gone from her back, shoulders, and head after many years in pain. Praise God.

The whole parish of Skt. Nikolaj Church in Esbjerg was touched and moved deeply from what took place among us through the ministry of Bob Canton and his wife Chita, and we are looking forward to having them back next year.

I, myself, was prayed over for the chronic disease morbus chron, and I believe the Lord has healed me instantly. Praise God.

With great joy and peace and thanks in my heart to Bob and Chita Canton. They are a great blessing to all the people here, especially Bob's great teachings and compassionate ministry."

—Rev. Fr. Benny Blumensaat, Esbjerg, Denmark—

"As I wasn't able to hear Robert Canton's talk at the Spiritual Warfare conference in September, since I was hearing confessions all weekend at the same time, I was listening to the audio CD of the talk while driving in my car last month in December. There is a part on CD #5 where he speaks about the blessings and graces of the sacrament of confession, and following that moment he asked about the name of the priests hearing confession and my name was mentioned. Shortly after that spot on the CD, he began speaking about people with lower and upper back pain. As he was speaking I could feel a loosening of tension in a key spot of my back that I had an injury in when I was a teen. It seemed as if he was talking directly to me in the CD and my back, in that particular spot, to this day feels better than ever since that day traveling and listening to the audio CDs. I feel that God has confirmed the healing ministry through this experience in my life and continues

to guide and open my heart to walking this path. My soul rejoices in the Lord and all the good things He has done for me. All glory and praise to Jesus Christ today and always, and blessings one hundred fold to those faithful and obedient to His Word."
—*Rev. Father Mark Sych, Edmonton, Alberta, Canada—*

"I want to thank you for all you've done for my family and me. Having been diagnosed with ALS last fall, your prayers have given me hope and stopped the progression of my disease. After each phone prayer, I have felt better and better. This is against what all the doctors have told me to expect. I want to thank you and the Lord again and again.

Also, two years ago, my brother–in-law was stricken with an unexplainable lung problem, with shortness of breath to the point of hospitalization. The doctors performed surgery to no avail. They were lost for what to do next. You prayed for him last December, and almost immediately he began to improve. In a very short time, he completely recovered. We attribute his miraculous healing from the Lord through your prayers. We all thank you."
—*Jean LB, Pacific City, OR—*

"My name is Bertha Lopez. I belong to Jesus. I attend the Blessed Sacrament Church in El Paso, Texas.

On February 4, 2011, my husband and I were invited to a Healing Retreat at Christ the Savior Church in El

Paso. Father Bill Halbing and Brother Robert Canton were guest speakers and healing ministers. At the first service on Friday night, Brother Bob said that the Lord was healing intestines, stomach problems and digestive system problems. He said that the Lord was melting away tumors or abnormal growths in the stomach area. I was prompted to go up front, but was a little hesitant; I had a navel hernia and I thought that it might not be for me, but the urge for me to go up front was very strong. I had had the hernia for ten years and even though I had been prayed over for it a number of times, and been asking God for a healing, it hadn't happened in all these years.

The doctors kept on telling me that they were going to do surgery on it, but it never happened. The reasons were that some of the doctors had moved out of town and also because I didn't have the money or the insurance to cover the cost. Finally, my latest doctor told me that what I needed was to lose weight and hopefully the hernia would shrink.

All this time I waited and nothing happened. The hernia kept growing, but it never hurt or bothered me at all. So I got used to it, until the night of the Healing Retreat. A few minutes after Brother Bob announced the healing, I immediately touched my abdomen and the ball or abnormal growth was not there anymore. It was big and hard, and suddenly it was gone! I felt like dancing at that very moment.

I was so elated that I wanted to shout out from the rooftop. Instead I went to tell Bob what happened to me, what the Lord did for me. The Lord can do it for you if you are willing to wait on Him. For He says in Isaiah 5:8-9, 'Your thoughts are not My thoughts and your ways are not My ways. As high as the heavens are above the earth, so high are My ways and My thoughts above your thoughts.' From that time on, I have kept on praising the Lord. He knows when, where, and how to heal us. He is never late. Amen."

—Bertha Lopez, El Paso, TX—

"Thank you very much for coming here in Perth, Western Australia. I am very grateful that I was able to come because in Jesus' Name, I am now completely a new person inside, and my back pain which I had for three-and-a-half years is totally healed. I thank the Lord for healing me and for making me a new person inside. Thank you very much, Brother Robert, to come as a servant of God and save so many souls and heal so many sick and those people who really needed the help of our Dear Lord. Thank you for being a servant of God to travel all over the world to proclaim the Good News and witness that our Lord Jesus Christ is Alive! Thank you very much to our Dear Lord Jesus Christ and thank you very much for ministering not only here in Perth but also in Sydney and Melbourne. Hope to see you again in Perth very soon. God bless you and all your family."

Your sister in Christ,

—Caroline Goumo, Perth, Western Australia—

"Glory be to Jesus Christ forever! I am writing my testimony of being healed through your prayers. I attended the ICCRS Leadership Training Course at Franciscan University in Steubenville, Ohio, where you were one of the main speakers in September 2010. During the last night's ecumenical healing service that was led by ICCRS at the Steubenville Urban Mission, you called out to the crowd through a word of knowledge that God wanted to heal someone from depression. I have had depression most of my life, ever since I can remember. I was already so blessed in my life by being a candidate for the Diaconate with the Ukrainian Catholic Eparchy of Edmonton (Alberta, Canada) and a part of this ICCRS Leadership Training Course with you. I wished that it was me that you were calling out to in the crowd, but I thought there had to be someone else that suffers more than I do, as I never ever thought that it could or would be me.

I walked up to the front for prayer a few minutes afterwards just to have you pray over me in a general way and receive a blessing from God and you, from the prompting and gifts of the Holy Spirit (without any kind of request from me), prayed over me to break the stronghold of depression by the Blood of Jesus Christ. You said to me through words of prophecy after 'My son, I love you! You have to love yourself, because I love you!'

Well, the song that was being played by the music ministry at that time was 'Open the Floodgates of Heaven – Let It Rain – Let It Rain' and God rained His love into my heart.

That night back in my room at the hotel, I could not stop singing praises to God. In fact, for the last month, I would wake up in the middle of the night, go to sleep, wake up in the morning, while in the shower, while driving, while just going for a walk, as I cannot stop singing praises to God.

This has never ever happened to me like this before in my life! That is how I know that I was healed – the fruits are good and are amazing, and I have truly been transformed!! It took God thirty-seven years to get through to my heart, but now I am madly, deeply in love with Jesus Christ. Truly, I have established a personal relationship with Him, and I am now living for Him alone!

The closest that I have ever felt like this before was for one week coming back from World Youth Day in Toronto in 2002 when I went to see Pope John Paul II, and for one month after going on a pilgrimage to Medjugorje, where Mary the Mother of God is allegedly appearing as the Queen of Peace. Now it has been over a month and not only is my depression gone and I am singing praises constantly without even thinking about it, the bondage that I was in with regards to temptation has drastically decreased big time I can honestly say, out of humility and thanksgiving, that I have been set free by Jesus the Divine Healer! Amen! Alleluia! Praise God!

Thank you, Brother Bob, for being His instrument in my healing!! I am sending you a CD of my Ukrainian Catholic Choir that I sang with for you and your wife, Chita, in thanksgiving for both of you! I pray daily and will continue to do so to support your healing ministry

in prayer. Please feel free to add this testimony to your website if you feel that it will bless someone else to reach out for Jesus' healing touch and be prayed for and with and by you."
—Marko S., Edmonton, Alberta, Canada—

"I began to feel sharp pain in my right elbow in February while I was in Sorocaba, Brazil. And it continued more and more frequently after I moved twenty boxes of books, each one with thirty to forty books in them, since I returned back home to Seoul, Korea.

So I went to get acupuncture treatments and to see a neurosurgeon for two months, since June. I felt that it was cured about 60 percent, especially with daily acupuncture, with more strength coming back in my right hand and wrist.

On October 8, I met Mr. Bob Canton to work with him as a translator for a retreat for 600 leaders of a charismatic renewal in Daegu City, Korea. It takes 2 hours to get there from Seoul by Express Train.

At about 7:30 A.M. he started to give his second talk, and I was interpreting for all of them. All of a sudden he began to caress his right arm with his left hand, saying, 'The Lord Jesus is touching and healing right elbows. Who is the person who's feeling the pain disappear?'

Right after translating the sentences, I raised my right arm, saying, 'Mine, too!'

The audience burst into clapping and alleluias, and several more people stood up with hands high in the air.

I knew it would happen at his retreat. Bob asked me to give my testimony at the start of his talk the next morning, so I was so happy and privileged to give my testimony for healing of the right elbow. That was the sixth miraculous physical healing that I've received from our loving Lord Jesus. Praise Jesus!"
—*Gemma Marie, OSB, Seoul, South Korea*—

"Brother Bob, I was trying to catch you at the Jakarta Grand Hyatt by phone. I left you a voice message. It was about the joyful news that my scoliosis was healed. Thursday, at the meeting you had with us: Genesis and St. Monica Prayer Groups primarily, I was one of those that you prayed over. Particularly at the exit door, you stepped back to pray for my scoliosis to be gone. I don't know how you knew about my scoliosis, since I did not tell you about it. Remember me, Beth Roxas?

After the meeting, I went to the Blessed Sacrament chapel to really just tell Him how happy and super joyful I was for all of the blessings that I have been receiving: Tuesday we were at the healing service with Sister Briege, then the unexpected, sudden session with you, and all the revelations of that morning session with you, that wonderful teaching about using our authority as baptized Christians and as leaders of the Renewal to serve and to protect the people of God from the enemy's attacks.

That Thursday, when we had our nightly Rosary, I noticed during the prayers that I could flex my left leg on the couch and do it at the same time as my right leg without any pain at all. This was unusual because the night before when I had attempted to do that I couldn't last a minute because of the pain. That did not surprise me because for the past so many years I already knew I couldn't do it anymore because of the scoliosis.

But this new development on Thursday night was surprising. After my spouse left the prayer room, I continued to test out my legs by sitting on the floor and now crossing them at the same time, like the Indian way or the way contemplative meditation formation is done, and I was able to do it, again and again. Tears started to trickle down my cheeks as I realized that healing had come to me. I was so overwhelmed with awe that God gave instant healing to me. I mean, that I didn't deserve to be healed so generously this way. I had stopped asking for healing of my scoliosis because osteoporosis was more serious to me. My doctor said that I could live with scoliosis, but the other would kill me silently. I was now thinking why did I ask for healing of scoliosis from you.

God knows what to do with me. When I heard you say so firmly: 'Let scoliosis be gone from her in Jesus' Name' in your prayer, I was convinced that you did a command prayer and, knowing how experienced you are, I felt that healing would come. But I did not expect it to be an instant healing. Lord, forgive my lack of belief. That's why I was so surprised to discover that I was able to cross my legs without pain. No pain at all.

Brother Bob, I am really so happy. Yesterday I went to Mass and really thanked Him, and for your intentions I prayed, as you asked us to pray for you, your ministry, and family always.

I hope I really am worthy to have the healing you powerfully ministered. Thank you for ministering to us and to thousands of people in Indonesia. Please do come back next year, and my prayer group wants to host you. We can hardly wait to hear your wonderful teachings.

Praise the Lord and I will always glorify Him. With heartfelt gratitude that we met, God bless!"

—*Beth Roxas, Jakarta, Indonesia*—

"I'm sending you my testimony and I thank God for your visit last November. I want to give God the glory for my healing and for you, Bob, a faithful servant for the Lord. When you laid your hands and prayed over me during the Healing Rally at Holy Cross here in Kauai, I could feel the blood in my veins moving throughout my body. I suffered from Sjogern Disease for thirty-six years, which is a chronic autoimmune disease in which a person's white blood cells attack their moisture glands. Also, last year my Lupus came back. I have been in remission with my Lupus after you prayed over me last November ,and the moisture has returned to my mouth and eyes.

Oh, give thanks to the Lord, for He is good! For His mercy endures forever. (1 Chr. 16:34)

I also thank you because you are a very powerful, yet very humble, instrument of the Lord. We are waiting for your return to Kauai before the end of this year."

—*Linda Silva, Kauia, HI*—

"I am writing to let you know how the good Lord, our Father, healed my son of autism. We were going frequently to the Children of God St. Luke's healing sessions since last year. My son, Denzel Martin, had been diagnosed with autism since he was three years old. When we immigrated to the United States when he was five years old, we got another formal diagnosis from a local California doctor.

Last year, after eight years, through the referral of the Valley Medical Regional Center, Martin underwent another assessment through the same doctor. Amazingly, that same doctor told us that Denzel had managed his way out of the autism spectrum disorder.

I believe in this miracle and the two comparable reports will document that the good Lord, our Saviour, has healed my son. With your prayers and by praying the Healing and Keeping prayer, which you shared with us, my son was saved from the claws of the enemy. It is with constant prayers, sacrifices, lots of faith, and hope that he was healed.

We, the parents, have to do our work and it was not an easy journey, but we know that we were never alone, that our Lord Jesus was walking with us. I want to proclaim to the world that Jesus is the greatest Healer, physician and friend. Please continue to pray for our family as we go on with this journey. Praise the Lord. Alleluia.

—Maria Duran, Stockton, CA—

"Friday, December 4, 2009—no more back pain. I attended the Kergyma Conference, a Catholic gathering, last weekend, and the final activity was a healing session with Brother Bob Canton. Brother Bob is a lay healing minister based in the United States and was invited to the Kergyma Conference.

Since I was seated at the Upper Box B Level of the Araneta Coliseum, I could not go down to the Ringside area where Brother Bob was. A lot of sick people were brought to him and he laid his hands on them.

A lot of miracles happened that day. The lame were able to walk, the deaf were able to hear, those with eye problems got clear vision back, and those with cancers and tumors were healed, and there were other healings.

Brother Bob reminded everyone that it was not he who heals but Jesus, and that he is just being used as an instrument of healing. Since Brother Bob could not possibly lay his hands on all of the 10,000 people gathered at the Araneta, especially those in the upper level of the coliseum, he said a special prayer of healing for all those who were present. He even said that we are all healers. Our faith in God can heal us of our infirmities. We just need to believe.

While saying his prayers, he said that he had a revelation that those with back pains will be healed. I had been suffering from back pains for weeks already. I knew it was the result of my poor posture and the stress I have at work. I was happy to hear that those with back pain will be healed. I touched my back, and I could still feel the pain. After I did that, I completely forgot about my backaches.

The next morning I remembered the Healing and Keeping prayer made by Brother Bob Canton given at the conference. I prayed it and it was a beautiful prayer, not only for physical healing, but also for emotional and spiritual healing.

When my boyfriend visited me in the afternoon he asked me about the conference and I excitedly told him how wonderful the conference was and about the miracles that happened.

While we were chatting, he placed his hand on my back, which he usually does to correct my posture and to give it a massage, because I always complain to him about my back.

I was surprised because when he touched my back I did not feel any ache at all. I touched my back just to be sure there was no pain and it did not hurt when I touched it. Actually, even if I don't touch my back, I can feel the pain in my back and up to my shoulders and neck almost on a daily basis.

There is already no back pain for me now and I can feel that my back is no longer a vulnerable part of my body unlike how it was before. It has been five days since the healing session and I still haven't had any back pain attacks. I am grateful to God for this blessing."

—Joy Anne P., Manila, Philippines—

"*I am in my late sixties and have been suffering from bad migraines for many years and have suffered often. Now they are gone. Jesus healed me instantly. Thank God.*

It is now April, and I have not experienced any of that pain. I am very glad. I believe in prayer and thank God for using Bob Canton to do His healing."
—Patrocinia Magaoay, Lanai City, HI—

"Dear Bob, Praise God for your talk to us at Holy Family Parish in Glendale, California. I left the service with a copy of the Healing and Keeping Prayer and decided to use it with full faith in God's Healing power. My dear friend called me crying because the doctors wanted to remove a cancerous breast. She was inconsolable, having just lost her mother. I said the Healing and Keeping Prayer with her on the phone and God's healing power shrunk her tumors and she is alive, well, and praising God. My charismatic prayer group prayed the Healing and Keeping Prayer for the aunt of one of our members. She has been in a coma for five weeks. She came out of it yesterday. Praise God again. I prayed that God would not take my friend's mother because they are the only two members of their family alive in the United States. She was rushed to the hospital last week with many complications from lung cancer (she never smoked a day in her life, but she sat next to her husband who smoked daily). I prayed to God using the Healing and Keeping Prayer and she was home the next day, resting comfortably.

Thanks again for visiting the parish. May God bless you and your ministry."
—Michael Roy, Glendale, CA—

"I am back to work in Prince George's County Public Schools! You know how glad I was when I drove to Pennsylvania Convention Center last June 1 and found out you were one of the speakers during the National Convention of Catholic Charismatics in the United States. Indeed I was healed, as my voice came back to normalcy (I was whispering when I talked to you before you conducted the Healing Service). This healing happened after I came back to present myself for the healing session on June 2. My doctor advised me to use a microphone should I come back to teach this year as media specialist in the county. That was bad news for me after the second operation to remove my right thyroid glands. He told me that normally the loss of voice is caused by fourth degree cancer on the thyroid glands, may last for several months, and would take a very long time until it would be back to maybe a near normal voice. After you laid your hand on me and I rested in the Spirit, I coughed away the hoarseness and started to sing audibly that same session. I gave a testimony right then and there about the goodness of God. That following Monday (since this happened on a Saturday) I answered a call from the school secretary for a document that she needed from me. I told her about what transpired in the Convention Center in Philadelphia that weekend. She commented that she could hear the normal and strong voice I now have and said, 'I hear the miracle in your voice!' All of my friends and even my doctor are amazed at how my voice came back to normal.

God be praised for blessing you with His Healing Gift!"
—*Jeogenes Biongcog, NJ*—

"In January 2012, I was diagnosed by an MRI with a completely torn rotator cuff. The doctor wanted to do surgery right away, but I wanted to attend the Southern Regional Conference of the Catholic Charismatic Renewal, so I scheduled my surgery for after the conference.

On Friday, March 23, 2012, in the afternoon at the Charismatic Conference, you were ministering through the charismatic gifts and gave a word of knowledge that God was healing a rotator cuff injury. I wasn't present at that time, but a friend, Ray Makofsky, mentioned it to me later in the day, and he prayed over my shoulder. During that prayer, Ray reminded the Lord of the word of knowledge that you received earlier about the healing of the rotator cuff. I felt heat going into the area. After he finished praying, I was amazed to find that I had use of my left arm and 'no pain' at all, whereas before I couldn't move that arm at all and I was in constant and excruciating pain.

When I went to the pre-operative appointment with my doctor, I told him all that had transpired. During his examinations, I could do everything with my arm that he wanted me to do and without pain. After the exam, the doctor gave me exercises to do to strengthen the muscles that were weak. They hadn't been used for three months because I wasn't able to move my arm from my side.

I asked the doctor if having the surgery would have given full range of motion as I have now. He said that after surgery and months of therapy, I would probably have regained most of the use of my arm, but not all (I'm sending you a copy of the doctor's report through the postal service). But thanks be to God, the Divine Physician said otherwise! I have complete range of motion and use of my arm, with no pain at all!

All glory to God!"

—Pat Clark, Kenner, LA—

"My dearest mother passed away on May 31, 2013. A couple of days after her funeral, our dear daughter Theresa brought me to Doctors Hospital ICU suffering from severe headache. I was unconscious. Later, she e-mailed my friend Eve informing her of my condition (brain hemorrhage) and asked for prayers. She then called you and found out you were out of state. Both of you prayed for me over the phone. At that moment, you told Eve that God's message to you was that I would be fine, and that there was nothing to worry about. I had a neurologist waiting for the scan results. He decided to wait until the next day for another scan before doing surgery. To his surprise, the bleeding stopped. It was a miracle! My neurologist told me that I was very lucky because most of his patients go to rehab afterward. I believe God healed me through your prayers. I was in the hospital for three days only. As of now, I am doing very well. Thank God for everything.

My family and I are forever grateful for all the prayers and love from you and your family. May our Dear Lord give you and your family members good health and more blessings to continue your ministries!"
—*Julie Gaspar, Stockton, CA*—

"*I am really glad to have received a copy of Bob Canton's Healing and Keeping Prayer from my auntie, Christina Ling. During those difficult times and running out of ideas when even the doctors in the hospital couldn't give me an exact answer and solution, I turned to the Healing and Keeping Prayer. I prayed very hard for my father, Philip Ling King, who was admitted to the intensive care unit. It was such a miracle that within three days my father showed signs of recovery and day-by-day he began to get stronger, better, and healthier. He has since been discharged from the hospital and is resting at home and on the road to recovery to his normal self. I, his son, Simon Ling, wish to extend my sincere thanks to the Robert Canton Ministries for the prayer. God bless you."*
—*Simon Ling, Singapore*—

Prayer for Healing
for Various Types of Diseases

Healing and Keeping Prayer

"Heavenly Father, I thank you for loving me. I thank you for sending your Son, Our Lord Jesus Christ, to the world to save and to set me free. I trust in your power and grace that sustain and restore me. Loving Father, touch me now with your healing hands, for I believe that your will is for me to be well in my mind, body, soul, and spirit. Cover me with the most precious blood of your Son, our Lord Jesus Christ, from the top of my head to the soles of my feet.

Cast out anything that should not be in me. Root out any unhealthy and abnormal cells and all causes of sickness from my entire body. Open any blocked arteries or veins and rebuild and replenish any damaged areas. Remove all inflammation and cleanse any infection by the power of Jesus' precious blood. Let the fire of your healing love pass through my entire body to heal and make new any diseased areas so that my body will function the way you created it to function. Fortify all my organs, all the systems in my body, all my arteries, blood vessels and veins, all my healthy tissues and cells, all my bones, joints, and ligaments, and all my nerves and muscles in my body by the power of your Holy Spirit. Touch also my mind and my emotion, even the deepest recesses of my heart. Saturate my entire being with your presence, love, joy, and peace and draw me ever closer to you every moment of my life.

And Father, fill me with your Holy Spirit and empower me to do your works so that my life will bring glory and honor to your holy name.

I ask this in the name of the Lord Jesus Christ, Amen."

Prayer for Empowerment

"Lord Jesus Christ, thank you for loving me, thank you for dying for me on the cross. Because of your death and resurrection you have redeemed and set me free. Have mercy on me, forgive me of all my sins. I surrender myself to you. I surrender to you my heart, my mind, my soul and my spirit, my will, my entire body and my entire being. I am totally yours and I give you permission to do unto me as you will. I invite you to come into my life and be the Lord and King and Savior and Deliverer and Healer of my life. I renounce Satan and all his empty works, and all his empty promises. Cover me Lord Jesus with your most precious blood from the top of my head to the soles of my feet, and protect me from the attacks and traps and tactics of the evil one. Send your Holy Spirit to strengthen and to empower me, to guide and to help me become more like you in every way. Come Holy Spirit and pour out on me your gifts and your fruit so that my life will give glory to the Holy Trinity. Mary, Mother Most Holy, and Mother of my Savior, Mother of God, Mother of the Messiah, pray for me throughout all the days of my life. Let the mantle of your love and healing and protection be upon me always. I also ask all the ministering angels in heaven, the angels of powers and virtues, the angels of healings and miracles, the angels of love and peace and joy, the angels of safety and protection, the angels of victory, Saints Michael, Gabriel, and Raphael and the archangels and legions of angels in heaven, to encamp around me and minister to me and to all my loved ones all the days of our lives. I ask all of these, in the mighty and powerful Name of Jesus, my Lord, Amen."

Spiritual Warfare Prayer

"Lord Jesus, you are my Savior and my deliverer. I thank you for dying for me on the Cross, because through your death and resurrection, you have set me free. I renounce right now any and all allegiance that I have ever given to Satan and his host of evil spirits. I resist them and I refuse to be intimidated or be used by them in any way whatsoever. I rebuke all their attacks upon my body, my emotion, my mind and spirit in the mighty name and by the power of the shed blood of the Lord Jesus Christ and through the mantle of Mary, the Immaculate Conception.

In Jesus' name, I break the transmission of any and all satanic vows, spiritual bonds, pacts, soul ties, and demonic works. I dissolve any and all curses, hexes, spells, traps, snares, obstacles, deceptions, lies, evil desires, evil wishes, hereditary seals, and every disease, infirmity, and affliction from any source including my mistakes and sins by the blood of Jesus.

In Jesus' Name, I break and dissolve any and all evil effects or ties associated with astrologers, clairvoyants, channelers, charters, crystals and crystal healers, mediums, fortune tellers, occult seers, palm, tea leaf, or tarot card readers, psychics, satanic cults, santeros, quack doctors, spirit guides, witches, witch-doctors, superstitious beliefs and practices, and the new age movement. By the precious blood of Jesus, I break and dissolve all effects of participation in seances and divination, Ouija boards, horoscopes, occult games, and any form of worship that does not offer true honor and recognition of the Holy Trinity and the Lordship of Jesus Christ. I stand secure upon the promises in the power of the Cross of Calvary whereby Satan and all his cohorts became defeated foes through the shed blood of the Lord Jesus Christ. I stand upon and claim all the promises of God's Word. In humble faith, I do here and now put on the whole armor of God that protects and enables me to do battle and to stand firm against the schemes and tactics of the evil one.

In faith, I cover myself, my loved ones, and all of our possessions with the precious blood of Jesus Christ.

Lord Jesus, I give you praise and honor and glory. You are the Victor over all evil and all glory belongs to you. Fill me now with your Holy Spirit and help me to become more like you. Mary, Help of Christians, I entreat you to place your mantle of protection upon me for you have crushed the head of the ancient serpent.

I also ask for the protection of the angels in heaven, the angels of powers and virtues and healings, the angels of love and joy and peace, the angels of safety and protection, Saints Michael, Gabriel, and Raphael and all the legions of angels to surround me and to minister to me and my loved ones all the days of our lives. I ask this in Jesus' Name and through the power of the Holy Spirit, Amen."

I encourage everyone to pray the "Healing and Keeping Prayer" every day, including the prayer for healing for specific type of sickness or disease. I would also like to recommend everyone to pray the "Prayer for Empowerment" and the "Spiritual Warfare Prayer" daily.

You may download a copy of these prayers by accessing my website at www.RobertCantonMinistries.org and distribute them to your friends and loved ones or to the sick. If you have some testimonies after reading this book, please send them to rccanton@sbcglobal.net for the greater glory and honor of God. God bless you!

—Robert C. Canton—